MONGOLIA

PRAEGER COUNTRY PROFILES

ROMANIA: *A Profile* by Ian M. Matley

PUERTO RICO: *A Profile* by Kal Wagenheim

Forthcoming
BURMA: *A Profile* by Norma Bixler

LUXEMBOURG: *A Profile* by Willard Allen Fletcher

TANZANIA: *A Profile* by John Hatch

PARAGUAY: *A Profile* by Charles J. Kolinski

NORWAY: *A Profile* by Vincent H. Malmstrom

FRANCE: *A Profile* by G. Etzel Pearcy

NICARAGUA: *A Profile* by Charles D. Stansifer and Mariano Fiallos

MONGOLIA
A PROFILE

Victor P. Petrov

PRAEGER PUBLISHERS
New York · Washington · London

PRAEGER PUBLISHERS
111 Fourth Avenue, New York, N.Y. 10003, U.S.A.
5, Cromwell Place, London S.W.7, England

Published in the United States of America in 1970
by Praeger Publishers, Inc.

© 1970 by Praeger Publishers, Inc.

Library of Congress Catalog Card Number: 69–19818

Printed in the United States of America

Contents

1	Introduction	3
2	The Natural Environment	10
3	Genghis Khan	21
4	From Genghis Khan to Tamerlane	29
5	From Tamerlane to Red Mongolia	39
6	Painful Growth	52
7	The Government	64
8	The Economy	70
9	Industries	77
10	Agriculture	88
11	Transportation and Communications	98
12	The People	106
13	The Arts and Recreation	123
14	Vanishing Customs	138
15	Foreign Relations	150
16	Mongolia—Today and Tomorrow	161
	Suggested Reading	171
	Index	175

A SECTION OF PHOTOGRAPHS FOLLOWS PAGE 56.

Maps

Relief   2

Railroads, Roads, and Industries   167

Population Distribution   168

Animal Husbandry and Farming   169

Administrative Divisions   170

MONGOLIA

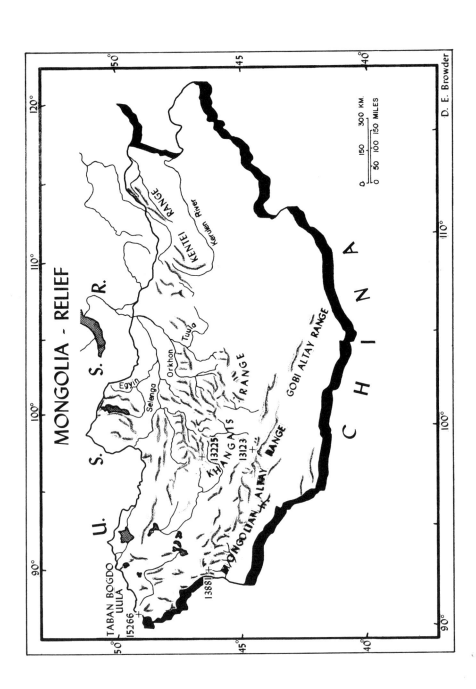

MONGOLIA - RELIEF

U. S. S. R.

CHINA

KENTEI RANGE

Kerulen River

Tuula

Orkhon

Selenga

Egyin

KHANGAI RANGE

GOBI ALTAY RANGE

MONGOLIAN ALTAY RANGE

TABAN BOGDO UULA
15266

13881

13225

13123

0   150   300 KM.
0 50 100 150 MILES

D. E. Browder

120°   110°   100°   90°

50°   45°   40°

1 Introduction

More than seven hundred years ago, Genghis Khan led his barbarian hordes out of Mongolia in the heartland of Asia to establish the largest empire the world has ever known. The bloodcurdling events of those days lie far in the past. We of the West tend to think of the Mongols as nomads, living in picturesque felt tents, tending their sheep, and herding their horses and camels and yaks on the edges of the great deserts of Central Asia. This is an accurate description of the Mongolian way of life of fifty years ago, but it is not representative of Mongolia today. Once again Mongolia has stepped forward to play a role in the world arena, not as a conqueror this time but as a pawn in the fascinating game of power politics.

Mongolia's new importance is due, first, to the natural resources of its forest-covered mountains, its fish-packed lakes, and its seemingly endless plains and deserts, and, second, to the fact that it is located between the two giants of the Communist world—the Soviet Union and Communist China. In an age of expanding populations and dwindling resources, both Russia and China covet this large land-locked reservoir of natural resources. It is not surprising that this nation of slightly more than 1 million Mongols looks with apprehension at the quarter of a billion Russians to the north and the three-quarters of a billion Chinese to the east, south, and west.

Because neither the Soviet Union nor Communist China can permit Mongolia to become a territorial part of the other, Mongolia has managed to maintain its independence for almost fifty years by playing one powerful neighbor against the other. This is not to say that the Mongols have not favored the Russians over the Chinese. The Mongols were subjects of the Chinese emperors from the end of the seventeenth century until well into the present century and often looked to their northern neighbors the Russians for assistance against the Chinese. With the aid of Soviet military units, Mongolia declared its complete independence from China in 1921, and it has existed independently as the Mongolian People's Republic ever since, albeit under strong Russian tutelage. In spite of the recent decentralization of Soviet power in Europe and elsewhere, Mongolia continues to lean heavily on Russian support and has taken the Soviet side in the ideological struggle between the Russian and Chinese brands of Communism.

Tremendous changes have occurred in Mongolia since 1921, when Mongolia was the most backward country of the Orient and its nomadic people knew so little of modern monetary systems that they preferred to use brick tea or hides as the medium of exchange. I remember a time spent among the nomadic Mongols. On pleasant summer evenings, I sat cross-legged outside felt-covered tents and drank numerous cups of Mongolian brick tea, which is brewed in a huge bowl and mixed with beaten eggs, butter, and milk and seasoned with plenty of salt—as unpalatable to the uninitiated as it sounds. But I remember too the delicious mare's milk offered to me by these gentle, hospitable heirs of Genghis Khan.

Old ways die hard, and most Mongols continue to live as their forefathers did centuries before, on the plains or in the mountains of this vast country. But the signs of change are not to be denied. Modern apartment developments on the outskirts of Ulan Bator, the capital of Mongolia, are giving some Mongols their first taste of modern living and of the benefits of electricity, modern heating plants, and plumbing. These people, few as they are, have taken a giant step forward into the twentieth century from a way of life little changed since the days of Genghis Khan.

Before we can understand the forces that have made such strides possible, we must know something of Mongolia's geography and history. The next chapter will be devoted to the landforms of the country, its climate, hydrography, vegetation, and other aspects of the environment, which has exerted such a great influence on the development of the land and people.

The story of Mongolia's past, told briefly in chapters 3, 4, and 5, includes some of the bloodiest but most exciting pages in the history of mankind, thanks to the military genius of Genghis Khan, a tribal chieftain who became ruler of an empire stretching from the Asian shores of the Pacific to the gates of Vienna and embracing most of European Russia as we know it today. Had the Mongolian invasion not occurred, the whole course of Russian history and Russian intellectual growth would have been entirely different.

Kublai Khan, grandson of Genghis Khan and the last of

the five great khans of the Mongol Empire, defeated and deposed the Chinese rulers of the Sung Dynasty and incorporated all of China into the Empire. He mounted the throne in Peking and founded the Yuan Dynasty, which lasted for almost a century. This interesting figure is known to the West largely through the writings of Marco Polo, the Venetian traveler and adventurer, who spent seventeen years in China, many of them in the service of Kublai Khan.

From the end of the seventeenth century until 1911, the territory of the Mongols was firmly ruled by the emperors of China. After the Chinese revolution, which overthrew the Manchu Dynasty in 1911, Mongolia declared its independence. Independence was short-lived, however, and, as a result of a treaty signed by China, Russia, and Mongolia, Mongolia became an autonomous part of the Republic of China and for all practical purposes a colony. The Russian civil war, which followed the Russian Revolution of 1917, spilled over into the hills and plains of Mongolia, and the White Russian general Baron Ungren von Sternberg, a former tsarist officer, declared himself ruler of Mongolia in order to protect it against the Red menace that he felt was about to engulf it. But Ungern and his small band of followers were defeated and taken to Siberia and executed. On July 11, 1921, Mongolia fell to the so-called Mongolian People's Government. Mongolia thus became the first state in Asia to be ruled by Communists outside the Soviet Union. The change-over to the Communist type of government was slow, however, and the country retained its traditional head of state until 1924. The present form of government and its Communist framework are discussed in Chapter 7.

In Ulan Bator and other large cities of Mongolia, industry was practically nonexistent in the early 1920's. Although the country is still a long way from being industrialized by American standards, great strides have been made in the development of industry. Startling changes are to be observed in rural Mongolia. The sight of former nomads concentrated in villages or growing crops on prairie lands where their herds once roamed free is even more indicative of modernization than are the signs of industrial progress. Chapters 8, 9, and 10 are devoted to economic development. To Western eyes these developments may not seem outstanding, but, when we compare them with economic conditions in Mongolia forty or fifty years ago, they seem truly spectacular.

Changes are also taking place in transportation. Early Mongol centers of administrative and religious life sprang up at the intersections of camel and horse trails. Many settlements are still connected by trails and narrow roads, which are now traversed mostly by cars and trucks, although camels are still very much in evidence. In 1950, the Trans-Mongolian Railroad was completed, connecting Ulan Bator with Russia to the north and China to the south. This and other developments in transportation and communication will be discussed in detail in Chapter 11.

Many Mongols live outside the Mongolian People's Republic. South and east of Mongolia proper, there are 1.3 million Mongols living as a national minority group in the Inner Mongolian Autonomous Region of China, generally referred to as Inner Mongolia. To the north, near Lake Baikal in Siberia, lives another concentration of people of

Mongolian origin, the Buryats. Members of these two groups are citizens of Communist China or of the Soviet Union and therefore fall outside the province of this book, but the people of the Mongolian People's Republic will be discussed in chapters 12 through 14. To understand these people we must be familiar not only with their ethnic background, the languages they use, and their religion but also with their houses, their living standards, the clothing they wear, the schools their children attend, their social organization, their culture, and their use of leisure. The changes brought about in the Mongolian people by the adoption of a new social system and the influence exerted upon them by the Soviet Russians are also described. For a quarter of a century after Mongolia became an independent nation, almost its only contact with the outside world was with the Soviet Union. This situation has changed somewhat. Recent developments in foreign relations are covered in Chapter 15.

Any reader who tries to understand the environmental, historical, political, economic, social, and cultural forces that are at work in Mongolia will need to have the answers to certain questions: Was the change-over from a nomadic society to the present Communist-dominated society a gradual evolutionary process, or did a revolutionary upheaval take place? What is the process that turns nomads with a primitive technology into industrial workers almost overnight? What made this almost completely illiterate, sleeping giant of a nation suddenly wish to become independent of foreign domination? Was it the memory of a glorious past, of the days of the great khans? Was it a desire to take part in the worldwide revolution concerned with the dignity of nations and of men as individuals?

Other questions of equal importance are asked in the concluding chapter. These questions have no simple, clear-cut answers. I hope that the reader will be able to answer them satisfactorily for himself when he has finished reading this book and that he will be better equipped to understand the changes taking place in modern Mongolia.

2 The Natural Environment

The Mongolian People's Republic sprawls over 591,119 square miles in the northern part of Central Asia. Three times as large as France, it exceeds in size the combined area of France, Spain, Portugal, Great Britain, and Ireland. Texas, with 267,339 square miles, has less than half the area of Mongolia. Alaska is the only U.S. state that exceeds it in size.

Mongolia measures 1,468 miles from east to west and 781 miles from north to south. It extends over 22 degrees of longitude and lies between the 41st and 52d parallels of northern latitude, approximately the same distance above the equator as France and the northern part of Spain. Its northern border with Siberia is 1,693 miles long. Its eastern, western, and southern borders, which it shares with Communist China, account for more than 60 per cent of the total border of some 4,360 miles. The northern frontiers follow high mountain ranges. The frontiers with China encounter no natural obstacles; they run through the Gobi Desert to the southeast and the Mongolian plains to the west. Perhaps the most significant geographical feature of the country is its relative isolation. Located in the approximate center of the Asian continent, it is separated from the other continents and the closest oceans and seas by tremendous distances.

Landforms

Until modern times, Mongolia was commonly thought of as a country of endless plains and prairies, over which the native nomads wandered with their herds, ever ready to answer the call of their military leaders to invade the neighboring regions. Even today most people are surprised to learn that Mongolia possesses vast mountainous and hilly areas and that it has a region where numerous lakes echo the beauties of Switzerland. Most surprising of all to the uninformed is the fact that the great steppes or plains in the eastern part of Mongolia occupy no more than 10 per cent of the entire area of the country. The existence of endless prairie lands is a myth.

When an astronaut looks down on Mongolia, the impression he has is of a vast mountainous area. The elevation ranges between 3,300 and 10,000 feet above sea level, with an average elevation of 5,000 feet. Practically all western, northern, central, and southwestern Mongolia is covered with hills, plateaus, and mountain ranges. The plateaus average between 3,300 and 6,600 feet in elevation. Even the so-called flat areas to the east are well above sea level; the lowest area, the Knock Noor Depression, has an elevation of 1,822 feet. The highest point in Mongolia is in the majestic Mongolian Altai Range to the west. This is Mount Tabun Bogdo Uula, which attains a height of 15,266 feet—not quite as high as Mont Blanc, the highest point in the Swiss Alps (15,781 feet), but higher than North America's Mount Whitney (14,494 feet) and the Swiss Matterhorn (14,690 feet). The mountain ranges of Mongolia are located in the western, southwestern, and northern parts of the country. The northern area, where rivers are abundant and the mountains and valleys are covered with forests, is termed *khangai*. In the north, the Kentei Range joins the Yablonovoy Range on the Russian side of the border, and the Khangai Range is integrated with the Eastern Sayan Mountains of Siberia. The Kentei Range gradually slopes down in an easterly and southerly direction, merging with the Gobi Desert to the south and with the Mongolian Plain to the east. The Plain has an elevation of between 1,920 and 2,640 feet, with occasional ranges of hills that reach heights of 3,960 feet above sea level.

The most formidable mountain system of Mongolia is located in the western part of the country. The Mongolian Altai Range begins in the extreme western corner from a mountain knot called Tabun Bogdo and stretches about 500 miles to the southeast. The Altai Mountains are on the average 12,540 feet high and 124 miles wide. The northeastern side of this range slopes gradually down and becomes a plateau. The southwestern side has extremely steep slopes. As the Mongolian Altai extends eastward, it becomes a series of low mountain ranges called the Bogi Altai, reaching 13,200 feet above sea level in the west but only 5,800 feet in the east.

Perhaps the most beautiful part of Mongolia is the Valley of Great Lakes, which is in the northwest, between the Khangai and Mongolian Altai ranges. The valley is almost completely surrounded by lofty mountain peaks and is dotted with numerous picturesque lakes.

Although southern Mongolia is usually associated with the Gobi Desert, it is not entirely desert. For centuries, the Mongolian word *gobi* has been misinterpreted by outsiders. Literally, *gobi* refers to the area in southern Mongolia that has little precipitation, sparse vegetation, and dry, parched land. The Gobi region is not a desert in the true sense of the word. Rather, it is a semidesert, without rivers. The Gobi Desert proper occupies no more than one-third of the entire Gobi region.

Climate

The climate of Mongolia in many ways differs from that of countries in other parts of the world lying within the same geographical latitude. This can be explained by the high elevation, the peculiarities of its relief, and its isolation. Mongolia is remote from oceans and seas and from ocean influences, which are blocked by mountain ranges. This results in a very dry climate with extremes in temperature between day and night and between winter and summer. The only other areas in the world with a similar high-altitude, continental climate are Tibet and Soviet Central Asia.

The average monthly temperatures of northern Italy, the Crimea, and the northern Caucasus, all located on the same average latitude as Mongolia, range from 32 ° F. in January to 68° F. in July. Mongolian winters are far more severe. Temperatures in January vary between 5° F. and −25.6° F. and occasionally drop to −49° F. or −58° F. on clear cloudless days with little snow. Temperatures in summer are just as extreme. The average in July fluctuates from 50° F. in the north to 77° F. in the south, where there are days as hot as 104° F. There is a range of 162° F. between extreme winter and summer temperature. The difference between day and night temperatures can be as great as 45° F.

Mongolia has not been blessed with sufficient precipitation in the form of either rain or snow. Annual precipitation varies from 4 to 14 inches and is distributed unevenly. Ulan Bator recorded 15.3 inches of precipitation in 1943 but only 5.5 inches in 1944, and similar conditions exist in other parts of the country, making agriculture a precarious occupation. On the whole, there is more precipitation in the north (10 to 14 inches) and less in the south, where it does not exceed 6 inches and sometimes is as little as 4 inches. Up to 90 per cent of the precipitation occurs in summer, often in the form of hail and sometimes in the form of torrential rains, in which a single day's downpour amounts to as much as one-half of the annual precipitation. In August, 1956, for example, the city of Dalan Dzadagad received 5.5 inches of rain within twenty-four hours. Winters are dry, with very little snow, which sometimes accounts for as little as 3 per cent of the annual precipitation.

Mongolia's remoteness from the ocean is responsible for the lack of precipitation. There is almost a complete loss of moisture in the air masses flowing south over the plains of Russia by the time the Mongolian border is reached. The country is blocked by high mountain chains to the north and west, so that the windward mountain slopes receive what moisture is left in the air masses, thus producing the northern and western forests, the luxurious grass cover, and the lakes. The leeward side of the mountains receives minimal amounts of moisture and consequently has an arid topography.

The severe winter climate and lack of snow cover cause the soil to freeze to unusual depths, with the result that much of Mongolia's subsoil, like that of Siberia, is permanently frozen. Parts of Mongolia that lie far south of Siberia have subsoils of this kind, called permafrost. The permafrost belt extends from Siberia to the central part of Mongolia, its southern border passing just north of Ulan Bator.

The seasons in Mongolia are sharply defined. Spring is never felt before April, when the temperature begins to climb above the freezing point. This is the season of strong winds and vicious sandstorms. The west winds blowing over Mongolia pick up huge quantities of sand particles and carry them eastward into Manchuria and northern China, completely blanketing with dust such cities as Peking, Tientsin, and Harbin. Summer lasts from June to the end of August. The month of July is especially hot. Autumn is the most favored season, with clear skies, fat cattle, and an abundance of mare's milk. Winters are generally cold, with high winds that blow away the insufficient snow cover. The absence of snow, even though it results in the soil's freezing to great depths, is beneficial to herdsmen because it permits cattle to graze the year round.

Rivers and Lakes

There are two classes of river in Mongolia: those that discharge into the Arctic and Pacific oceans, along the Russian and Chinese coasts respectively, and those that drain into the landlocked lakes and plains and deserts of Mongolia and Central Asia. Surprisingly enough, most Mongolian rivers belong to the latter class and drain into the large enclosed basin that constitutes about two-thirds of the total area of Mongolia. These rivers are swift and unruly. Many of them flow through gullies in the mountains and represent vast water-power resources. The rivers that flow into the eastern plains are placid and slow and have little water-power potential.

The most important navigable river of Mongolia is the Selenga, which flows north and collects its waters from about one-sixth of the entire area of the country. After it leaves Mongolia, the Selenga flows into the Soviet Trans-Baikal region, where it empties its water into Lake Baikal and discharges into the Arctic Ocean by way of the Angara and Yenisei rivers. The sources of the Selenga River are on the slopes of the Khangai Mountains. Its basin comprises 164,000 square miles altogether, of which two-thirds are located in Mongolia and one-third in Russian Siberia. The Selenga's total length is 748 miles; the river courses through Mongolia for 650 miles and is fully navigable for 294 miles upriver from the Mongolian-Russian border. Other rivers flowing into the Arctic are the Hara near Ulan Bator, the Yoroo to the west of the Kentei Range, and the Orkhon, a tributary of the Selenga, which is 697 miles long and has a basin of 51,350 square miles.

Two Mongolian rivers that flow into the Pacific Ocean are important: the Onon and the Kerulen, both of which have their sources on the slopes of the Kentei Range. The Khalkha, a third river flowing into the Pacific, has its sources in the Great Khingan Range in eastern Mongolia.

Several important rivers flow into the landlocked basin of Central Asia, among which are the Kobdo and Dzabkan. Neither is very long, and both come to an end in the lake district of Mongolia. The Gobi region is practically devoid of rivers, except for the Ongin Gol, which is 270 miles long, and the Tuyin and Baydarag rivers, which begin on the slopes of the Khangai plateau and disappear in the sands of the Gobi.

Mongolia is blessed with many lakes, especially in the northwest. Upsa Nur, at the northern end of the Valley of Great Lakes, is the deepest and largest fresh-water lake in the country. It has an area of 1,293 square miles and is 785 feet deep. Several large lakes in the Valley of Great Lakes have no outlets and are therefore mostly salt water. The largest are Hara Nur, Hara Usa, and Hirgis Nur. Perhaps the most picturesque lake in Mongolia is Khubsugul, which is located in the extreme northern part of the country and is surrounded by high mountains. It has an elevation of 5,280 feet, is supplied by no less than forty-six rivers, and has an area of 1,012 square miles. There are also several lakes in the remote eastern part of the country. Buir Nur, with an area of 235 square miles, is the largest of these.

In spite of an abundance of rivers and lakes, Mongolia suffers from a shortage of water. During severe winters, water sources freeze for five or six months, and the population and livestock must depend on snow and ice for their water supply. Only one-third of the country has sufficient surface water; another third depends on underground water; the final third has neither surface nor ground water in adequate amounts.

Soil and Vegetation

Northern Mongolia has black soil and soils of the chestnut type, both of which are good for agriculture. Southern Mongolia is mostly salt flats mixed with sand and some brown soils. The types of vegetation found in Mongolia vary according to relief, climate, latitude, and elevation. Six well-defined vegetation zones can be distinguished:

Alpine. Scrubby bushes and grasses that thrive at high altitudes are found at elevations between 6,500 and 10,000 feet in northern and northwestern Mongolia, mostly in the Eastern Sayan, Khangai, and Mongolian Altai ranges. These alpine meadows provide good grazing land for cattle.

Mountain Taiga. Vegetation of the taiga type consists of dense coniferous forests with a limited grass cover. This zone occupies a comparatively small area in the northern part of the Khangai Mountains and in the Khubsugul Lake region, at an elevation of about 6,000 feet.

Mountain Steppe and Forest. About one-fifth of Mongolia is occupied by deciduous forests and mountain steppes with good grass cover suitable for grazing. This zone is mostly situated in the mountain regions of the northern part of the country.

Steppe. Vegetation of the steppe, or prairie, type covers considerable areas of Mongolia, especially in the east. About 90 per cent of the steppe area is excellent grazing land.

Semidesert. The vegetation of this zone is represented by coarse grasses of the feathergrass variety, mainly in the northern part of the Gobi region and in the Valley of Great Lakes.

Desert. A relatively small area of southwestern Mongolia, on the fringes of the great Central Asian desert, is characterized by extreme dryness and very poor soils or no soil at all. Vegetation, when it exists, is of the hardy tamarisk varieties, Gobi rhubarb, and brush.

Almost two-thirds of the entire territory of Mongolia have excellent grazing lands. However, the forests are important in the economy of the country, not only commercially but also for the part they play in storing and protecting the country's water resources. Few people outside Mongolia realize that the country's forest resources are among the largest in East Asia from the standpoint of available timberland and per capita forest reserves. Figures published in Moscow in 1964 revealed that, among the four countries of East Asia for which figures were available (Mongolia, North Vietnam, North Korea, and Communist China), Mongolia was second only to Communist China in total area of timberland reserves. The large timberland acreage per capita in Mongolia reflects the high ratio of land to people. Although Mongolia's timberland area is vast, it occupies only 9 per cent of the entire area of the country. In Communist China, forest lands occupy 8.6 per cent of the area.

Trees in the timberlands of Mongolia are mostly conifers (about 90 per cent), among which the most predominant are the larch (72 per cent of total forest trees) and the Siberian pine (12 per cent).

Fauna

The animal life of Mongolia is most varied in the forest and mountain regions, where fur-bearing animals such as sable, ermine, otter, and squirrel, as well as several varieties of wild hoofed animals, such as musk deer, roe deer, moose, and Siberian stag, are found in abundance. Reindeer, less numerous, are found principally in the Lake Khubsugul region; beaver, in the vicinity of the Khobdo River. The tarbagan, a small rodent resembling a marmot, is widely distributed over the prairie lands of Mongolia and is hunted for its fur, which has great commercial value as an export. Wild birds abound in the forests and steppes. The largest is the *drofa,* a variety of wild turkey. Mongolia's rivers and lakes attract large numbers of migratory birds, especially geese and ducks. The western regions have many pheasants.

The semidesert and desert regions support a few wild species that are becoming quite rare—horses, asses, and, in smaller numbers, camels. Wild asses are found mainly in the southwest, and wild horses, called Przhevalsky horses after the Russian explorer who first described them in 1883, are found in the Bulgun River region.

This, then, is a picture of the land from which the Mongol conquerors set forth on their forays into Asia and Europe centuries ago—a land of extremes, with an inadequate water supply.

3 Genghis Khan

Mongolia did not become a political entity until the sixteenth century. Before that time its size was ever changing, like an inflated, then deflated, balloon. Its shape also changed; the area was frequently fragmented into several small principalities at war with one another. The coming of Genghis Khan resulted in the first reliable descriptions of Mongolia and its history. The first of the great khans ordered that records be kept of all important events occurring during his reign, and because of his foresight the subsequent history of Mongolia is fully documented. The history of Mongolia before his reign is not so well known.

According to legend, Mongolia was settled in prehistoric times by people with long heads, red hair, and green eyes. In Neolithic times, the area was occupied by small groups of hunters and nomads. The Huns settled in Mongolia in the third century A.D. They were followed by the Turkic people, who held sway from the sixth century A.D. to the eighth. During A.D. 745–840, the Uigurs formed an empire in the area. The Uigurs were peaceful people who seldom engaged in military campaigns against their neighbors except to protect their territory from invaders. Their state was one of the most stable of those days, but it was not destined to last. At the beginning of the tenth century, the Uigurs were conquered by the Kirghiz tribes, which swooped down on Mongolia from the Yenisei River in the north. The last people to occupy the area before it fell to the Mongols were the Khitans.

Genghis Khan, carrying on the work of his father, welded the dispersed, wandering Mongol tribes into the conquerors of a mighty empire. Undoubtedly a military genius and skilled in tribal politics, he created an empire that eventually spread from the shores of the Pacific in the east to the Adriatic Sea in the west, and from Siberia in the north to the countries known today as Vietnam and Burma in the south. Neither the magnificent campaigns of Alexander the Great of Macedonia nor those of Julius Caesar and the Roman emperors that came after him can match the military campaigns of Genghis Khan. Even the conquests of Napoleon fail to match in size the territories that were literally trampled under the hooves of the horsemen of Genghis Khan and his descendants. Whole cities were wiped off the face of the earth. Thousands upon thousands perished. When we consider that there are no more than 3 million Mongols living today, thinly spread out over the present Mongolian People's Republic, the Inner Mongolian Autonomous Region of China, and the Trans-Baikal areas of Russia, on land that is largely steppes and deserts, we find it hard to believe that the ancestors of this relatively small group of men were able to conquer the once mighty empires of China and Persia and to occupy the vast lands of Russia.

The Young Temuchin

Temuchin, as Genghis Khan was called in his youth, was probably born in February, 1167. We are told that, as a youth, Temuchin was very tall and that he had a broad forehead and long beard. Many years after his death, it was reported that he had been born with gray eyes and fair hair like the other children of his father, Yesukai. These features alone would distinguish him from the typical, dark-haired Mongol. We have no way of knowing if he was a pure-blooded Mongol or a descendant of the legendary green-eyed, long-headed peoples of an earlier day, but we do know that the children of Genghis Khan were fair-haired and gray-eyed and that he was more than a little concerned when his grandson Kublai was born with the dark hair characteristic of most Mongols.

Yesukai, Temuchin's father, ruled a small tribe of Mongols living on the Onon River near the northeastern corner of Mongolia, about six miles north of the present border of the Soviet Union. When Temuchin was eight or nine years old, his father was poisoned; the mantle of leadership eventually fell on young Temuchin's shoulders. In his formative years, he had to deal not only with leaders of other tribes but also with members of his immediate family, as well as with distant relatives. Many years of fratricidal strife followed, during which Temuchin did his best to unite the warring Mongol tribes into a single nation. Finally, in 1206, the Mongol princes and rulers assembled on the banks of the Onon River with their retinues and selected Temuchin their leader, bestowing upon him the name of Genghis (it is sometimes spelled Jenghiz, Chingis, and Chinggis) Khan.

The tribes consolidated by Genghis Khan were poor. Like most nomadic groups, they found it difficult to accumulate riches while constantly moving from pasture to pasture, but under their aggressive leader, they lost no time in acquiring the riches of less nomadic neighbors, some of whose cultures had been developing for centuries. In 1207, the new Mongol nation embarked on a series of invasions.

Years of Conquest

Genghis Khan's first victims were the complacent, un-warlike tribes that lived north of the Selenga River and in the Yenisei River Basin. The wealth acquired from them was used to equip the Mongol armies for the invasion of the land of the Tanguts, who had set up a well-established state in Central Asia, south of modern Mongolia. The Tanguts were completely overrun by the fast-moving hordes of horsemen and were forced to pay tribute to their rampaging conquerors.

Two years later, in 1209, the Uigurs in eastern Turkistan, just west of Mongolia, were confronted by the Mongols. After a series of bloody battles, the state of the Uigurs was made part of Mongolia. Having brought his neighbors immediately to the north, west, and south under the Mongolian yoke, Genghis Khan set his sights on northern China, one of the most civilized areas of the time. Two years were spent in preparations for the onslaught, which came in 1211. A humiliating defeat was inflicted on the Chinese forces of the Chin Empire in northern China by the united Mongol and Tatar forces. The Mongols occupied the capital city of Peking in 1215. In the following years the Chin Empire was reduced to the status of a buffer state between the Mongols to the north and the Sung Empire to the south.

Genghis Khan's next major move was to the southwest, in the direction of the flourishing Khorezm (Khwarizm) Empire in Central Asia, east of the Caspian Sea. The states of this empire had been powerful and rich enough to attract Alexander the Great, who had passed through the region seventeen centuries before Genghis Khan. They were still rich in natural resources and boasted a trade that flourished far and wide in all the countries of the known world.

The destruction of Khorezm was caused, in part, by the Khorezmians themselves. Genghis Khan sent emissaries to seek trading agreements. Having received the pledge of the Shah that Mongol traders could travel to Khorezm unmolested, he dispatched trading caravans, one of which was stopped at Otrar. The Mongols were arrested under the pretext that spies were among them, and every member of the 150-man caravan was put to death by orders of the Shah. Genghis Khan then sent a mission to the Shah, demanding that the governor of Otrar be punished for the massacre. The Shah summarily executed the head of the mission and sent the other members of the mission back in dishonor after burning off their beards.

The punishment inflicted by the Mongols on the Khorezm Empire for these outrages rivals in cruelty the worst depredations of modern warfare. At some time during the last months of 1220 and the first months of 1221, this ancient empire was conquered. Its towns and cities were ravaged, its gardens and fields laid waste, its irrigation system was destroyed. The cities of Bukhara and Samarkand were leveled and their inhabitants murdered or (if they were artisans) enslaved. The final battle on the banks of the Indus River sealed the fate of the Khorezm Empire. For centuries, the region suffered from the effects of the Mongol invasion.

While Genghis Khan was laying to waste the rich and venerable Khorezm Empire, other Mongols were overrunning Persia and heading northward into Transcaucasia, between the Black Sea and the Caspian Sea. The Christian Georgian knights were defeated, and the Mongols moved north along the shores of the Caspian Sea as far as the southern steppes of present-day Russia. Subutai, the most skilful of Genghis Khan's generals, met the Russians there for the first time.

The Russians repeated the mistakes made by the Khorezmians. When Subutai's envoys appeared at the Russian camp, offering peace if the Russians would not protect the Cumans (old enemies of Russia who were seeking Russian assistance against the Mongols), the Russian princes responded by executing the envoys. The result was the same as it had been in Khorezm. Although the Russians outnumbered the Mongols and fought valiantly, they were poorly organized. Their troops had been assembled from feudal principalities and acted independently. Without a unified command or battle plan, they were defeated at the Kalka River not far from the Sea of Azov in the year 1223. Six princes lost their lives in the battle. When it was over there was no Russian army left to stem the Mongol invasion.

And then the incredible happened. The victors, instead of pursuing the Russians into the rich cities lying to the west and northwest, simply marched away and disappeared into the steppes to the east. This was a welcome respite for the Russians, one that might have changed the course of history if the Russians had taken advantage of it by uniting and preparing for the next onslaught, which they had every reason to believe would come. But five years went by and nothing was done; then ten years slipped by, and the Mongols were forgotten.

Genghis Khan in the meantime had returned to Karakorum, the capital of his empire, but he was not to remain there for long. In 1226, he was on the march again, southward this time, to subdue the Tanguts, who had become restive and were attempting to throw off the Mongolian yoke. The new invasion was even more destructive and bloody than that of 1207. When it ended, ruins, desolation, and the stench of death were all that remained of the state of the Tanguts.

End of an Era

What was the secret of the Mongols' invincibility? It was not the strength of the Mongols so much as the weakness of their opponents. They were usually agriculturalists and city dwellers and were thus particularly vulnerable to the hit and run tactics used by the attackers. Invariably, they were disunited, at odds with each other, and often willing to help the Mongols defeat neighboring groups in the hope that they themselves would not become victims. But without the superior military organization built up by Genghis Khan, the Mongols would not have been as successful. The first of the great khans had developed a well-organized, highly mobile force of horsemen who could travel at amazing speed and carry their supplies with them. Tactically, they had several advantages. One was the location of the command post in battle. Mongol commanders, whether they were commanding a hundred warriors, a thousand, or ten thousand, directed the battle from behind the lines, usually on an elevation from which they could observe the progress of battle and issue commands as needed. The leaders of their opponents led their troops into battle, ready to conquer or to die with their warriors. From a military point of view, this gallant show of bravery was unwise. The Mongols were usually armed with bows and arrows, which could be aimed at a leader from a distance, and sometimes with spears equipped with hooks capable of dragging an adversary off his horse.

Another great tactical advantage was denied to enemies of the Mongols. After the conquest of China and Persia, hundreds of Chinese and Persian engineers, skilled in the art of siege, served as auxiliary troops and introduced catapults for hurling heavy rocks and siege ladders, battering-rams, and other sophisticated devices for scaling walls and breaking down the gates of walled cities.

In 1227, while he was engaged in leveling the state of the Tanguts to the ground, Genghis Khan died. Two years later, the leaders of the various Mongol tribes gathered at Karakorum to elect the new great khan from among his surviving sons.

Meanwhile, the Russian princes continued to quarrel and squabble among themselves, in blissful ignorance of the fact that they were soon to feel the Mongol yoke and were to endure it for the next 250 years. Genghis Khan was dead, but the mighty military machine he had created was still very much alive. A new era in the history of the Mongols was about to begin.

4 From Genghis Khan to Tamerlane

Genghis Khan had four sons. The eldest, Juji, died two years before death claimed the great khan himself. Before dying, Genghis Khan had made it clear that the throne should go to Ogadai, the second oldest of his surviving sons; but the *kurultai* (great council) that convened at Karakorum in 1229 was to choose the successor. It was a difficult choice. In addition to the dead khan's sons and grandsons, all his near relatives were present in the capital. After a prolonged series of discussions and arguments, Ogadai was chosen to be the next great khan.

The Golden Horde

At the time that the *kurultai* elected Genghis Khan's successor, it decided to entrust an invasion of southern Russia to Batu, who was the son of Juji and who was to go down in history as the conqueror of Russia and the Mongol leader whose name struck terror into the hearts of the peoples of Europe. An attempt to invade the lands to the west had already been made in 1226–27, when Batu, with the aid of the forces of Subutai, swept through the land of the Volga Bulgars, while the lands of the Cumans north of the Black Sea were being laid waste by Batu's cousins, Kuyuk and Mangu.

The earlier campaign had met with indifferent success, however, and the *kurultai* of 1229 decided that Batu was to subdue not only the Cumans and Bulgars but some of the Russian principalities as well. Unlike most of the preceding Mongol invasions, this was not to be a concerted effort of all the Mongols but was to be limited to what Batu could achieve with the horsemen of his own *ulus*. (Batu, on his father's death, had inherited Juji's *ulus*—equivalent to the fiefs held by feudal nobles who swore fealty to the kings of Western Europe.) Batu's collective *ulus* were eventually to constitute an empire, but his forces were not then sufficient to carry out the task assigned to them, and the campaigns of 1230–32 were far from a spectacular success.

In the meantime, Great Khan Ogadai had completely destroyed the rule of the Chin Dynasty in northern and central China. All China, with the exception of the southern part ruled by the Sung Dynasty, was now in Mongol hands. In 1235, Ogadai summoned a new *kurultai,* and the decision was made to utilize all the forces of the Mongol Empire in an attempt to invade and occupy the countries to the west. This was a fateful decision for Russia. Before the Mongol invasion, Russia was one of the most enlightened countries in Europe, and its ruling princes were related by marriage to every important European royal house. Under the whips of the Mongol horsemen, it was to become one of the most stagnant and backward nations on the continent.

Preparations for the invasion were thorough. The decision of the *kurultai* was made known in every corner of the Mongol Empire. Subutai, the most fearsome of Genghis Khan's generals, was recalled from China. During 1235 and 1236, the Mongolian forces gradually collected in the upper reaches of the Irtysh River and in the vicinity of the Altai Mountains. In the winter of 1237–38, this enormous group of men started to move westward. It was an awesome sight—thousand upon thousand Mongol horsemen and auxiliary troops enlisted from subjugated countries, followed by an almost endless line of horse-drawn wagons. They were joined by additional troops from regions along the way, which had previously been conquered by the Mongols. It was invasion on a grand scale. The total force numbered 120,000 to 140,-000 warriors, of which no less than 50,000 were Mongols.

The capital of the original Russian state was Kiev, the "mother of Russian cities," but the Grand Dukes of Russia had transferred their official residence from Kiev to Vladimir in the northwest. This rich and prosperous region was the first goal of the Mongols. Wars usually were conducted in the summer, but the invasion had been planned for winter, when the rivers were frozen and the cavalry could easily cross the water barriers between Mongolia and northwest Russia. The Mongols' planning paid off. The Russians were caught unprepared.

Batu, with his enormous horde, headed for the city of Ryazan. Every town on the way was captured and razed. The fate of Izheslavets was typical. It was so devastated that it was never to rise from the ruins. Most of the defenders were slain. Neither women nor children were spared. The only men spared were artisans, who were sent as slaves to the banks of the lower Volga, where Batu was later to administer his empire, which came to be known as the Golden Horde because of the magnificence of the conqueror's tents.

In later days, when people spoke of the Golden Horde, they referred to Batu's empire rather than to his conquering hordes.

City after city, town after town fell to the sabers of the Mongols and were put to the torch. After capturing Ryazan, the cavalry hurried on toward Vladimir. A chain of destruction was forged between Ryazan and Vladimir. Moscow, then scarcely more than a town, was among the many small cities that were burned to the ground. Vladimir was reached on February 4, 1238, and the siege began on February 6. Heavy siege weapons, capable of hurling huge rocks at the walls and towers of the fortified city, were drawn up. Vladimir fell the next day. Its defenders were massacred, and the city was completely destroyed. The family of the Grand Duke, his retinue, and several high-ranking officers refused to surrender and sought refuge in the Uspensky Cathedral. The cathedral became their flaming tomb.

For some reason, two of the greatest, richest, and most famous Russian cities—Novgorod and Pskov—were spared. The explanation may lie in the fact that the progress of the Mongols was blunted by the stubborn resistance put up by many cities and towns. At any rate, as the spring thaw approached, and the Mongolian cavalry, concerned about maneuverability in the muddy quagmire of the northwest region, turned back. A meeting of the *kurultai* was called, and a decision was made to move south and west. The Mongolian horde, increased many times in size by the addition of plunder and thousands of prisoners urged on by the Mongols' whips, turned south toward Kiev.

Nothing, it seemed, would stop the inexorable drive toward the ancient capital of Russia. However, progress was delayed for two months by resistance from the insignificant town of Kozelsk, southwest of Moscow. Great cities like Vladimir had fallen under the blows of Mongol catapults and battering-rams in a matter of days, but for weeks stubborn little Kozelsk fought off the invaders with bows, arrows, rocks, and hot oil. When the Mongols finally breached the walls, the defenders plugged the broken walls with the bodies of dead Mongols. They even dared to make forays into the attackers' ranks and succeeded in destroying a number of catapults. But this brave effort was their last. The defenders of Kozelsk were finally engulfed by the Mongols. None were spared; blood of young and old flowed freely in the river that ran through the town.

The rest of 1238 was spent in raids on the Crimean Peninsula and the north Caucasian lands of the Circassians. During the next two years, the Mongols drove westward, overrunning several ancient cities and towns. In December, 1240, they laid siege to Kiev. After nine days, the city fell. It was many decades before the capital recovered its political and commercial importance.

The conquest of Russia was virtually complete. With the exception of the far northwest, the entire country lay in ruins. The hordes of Batu Khan pushed on into Eastern Europe. At the battle of Liegnitz in Poland in 1241, the combined force of Polish and German knights was completely annihilated. The knighthood of Hungary met the same fate. The road to Vienna and all of Western Europe lay open.

Then Great Khan Ogadai died, and, with the exception of the troops commanded by Batu, the Mongol forces were withdrawn. Batu did not have enough forces to continue the drive westward, and Europe was spared. Batu contented himself with burning and pillaging the buffer areas west of Russia; then he returned to his headquarters on the lower reaches of the Volga, where he set about administering the empire of the Golden Horde.

The Heirs of Genghis Khan

The second of the great khans, Ogadai, died on December 11, 1241. A contemporary historian noted sadly that Ogadai had been too addicted to hunting, drinking, and women. An interregnum followed; then in 1246 another *kurultai* elected Ogadai's son Kuyuk as the new great khan. When Kuyuk died two years later, the descendants of the four sons of Genghis Khan engaged in a power struggle that brought the great empire of the Mongols to the brink of civil war. The rivalry was most keen between the descendants of Ogadai and Tuli. When Batu, son of Juji, joined the struggle, he leaned toward the Tuli faction, with the result that the mantle fell on the shoulders of Mangu, Tuli's eldest son, who ruled as great khan from 1251 to 1259.

The reign of Mangu is significant in one respect: with the exception of Timur, who ruled from 1294 to 1307, he was the last recognized ruler of the widespread Mongol Empire. At his death in 1259, his brother Kublai became the fourth great khan but for all practical purposes ruled only China and Mongolia. By the time of Kublai, the empire of Genghis Khan had devolved into three mighty empires, each completely independent of the other: Batu's empire, the Golden Horde, included all of Russia; Kublai's empire embraced China as well as all of Mongolia with the exception of the western regions adjoining Batu's empire; the empire of Hulagu, the brother of Kublai and Mangu, who defeated the Caliph of Baghdad in 1258, was in Persia and the neighboring states, where Hulagu had founded a new Mongolian dynasty in 1261.

With each succeeding generation, the ruling dynasties became further separated. After a century and a half, fratricidal conflict and civil war brought all three empires to an end. While they endured, the Mongol empires included most of the known world. Only that small appendix of the Eurasian continent known as Western Europe remained free of Mongol domination. It is amazing, in spite of the spectacular nature of the conquests of the Mongols and the extent of their empire, how little Western Europeans knew of the lands ruled by the Mongols. Western Europe was the center of the universe to its own inhabitants, and the East was largely unknown to them until Marco Polo's account of his years in the service of Kublai Khan.

Kublai Khan

Of the various great khans and lesser rulers of the vast empire of the Mongols, three were outstanding: Genghis Khan, whose story we have already told; Tamerlane, whose bloody reign will be described in the next chapter; and Kublai Khan, who established the Yuan Dynasty in China.

Kublai, third son of Genghis Khan's son Tuli, was proclaimed great khan of the Mongolian Empire in 1260, while he was conducting a military operation in the province of Chahar in China. Apparently, Hulagu, his older brother, was not elected because he had been entrusted with the job of conquering and administering Persia and was thousands of miles away in the Middle East when the *kurultai* was convened.

Upon ascending the throne, Kublai was immediately challenged by his younger brother Arik-Buka, and for several years the empire of the Mongols was aflame with war waged by descendants of Genghis Khan, all of whom coveted the throne. Besides Arik-Buka, the principal contenders were Bereke, son of Juji (first son of Genghis Khan), and Algu, grandson of Jagatai (second son of Genghis Khan). Although Kublai was elected great khan in 1260, it was not until 1266, when Bereke, the last of the contenders, died, that Kublai could proclaim himself sole ruler of the empire. Arik-Buka died the same year. Algu had died in 1265, as had Hulagu. By this time, there were three empires instead of one. Kublai had already transferred his capital to Peking and was to devote the rest of his life to enlarging and administering the huge eastern empire of the Mongols.

Kublai's interest in China and its destiny stemmed from the fact that he had been educated by Chinese scholars brought to the court in Karakorum. He was the first of the descendants of Genghis Khan to abandon shamanism, the religion of his ancestors, and adopt Buddhism. Kublai's Buddhism, however, was a mixture of shamanism and Buddhism. The religion that evolved from this combination was finally known as Mongolian Lamaism.

Twice Kublai attempted to extend his kingdom eastward by invading Japan, first in 1274 and again in 1281, failing each time because of divine intervention in the form of great typhoons that destroyed his invading armadas. However, he did succeed in extending the borders of his empire as far south as Burma and Indochina, but not until he had dealt a final blow to the tottering Sung Dynasty, which had held south China in sway. The dynasty was shattered in 1280, and its lands were added to the Mongol Empire. Upper Burma was conquered in 1283–84, followed by Indochina, Malacca, and Java. Kublai made no attempt to extend his borders westward because all the lands to the west were ruled by his relatives, descendants of the first of the great khans.

The Yuan Dynasty, founded by Kublai Khan in 1271, lasted for less than a hundred years. Most of Kublai's successors lacked the ability to govern so huge an empire. The exception was his grandson Timur, who ascended the throne in 1294 after Kublai's death. Timur inherited the title of great khan, and during his thirteen-year reign was recognized by all parts of the empire as ruler of the Mongols. At the time of Timur, the empire extended as far west as the Dnieper River in Russia and as far south as the Ganges in India.

Timur was succeeded by six emperors whose combined reign lasted no more than twenty-five years and whose principal preoccupations were wine, women, and luxury. Toghon-Timur, the last ruler of the dynasty founded by Kublai Khan, ruled for thirty-five years (1333–68) before popular revolt spread through China, resulting in the capture of Peking by insurgents and the founding of the popular Ming Dynasty in 1368. The Ming Dynasty was to endure for the next three centuries, thus ending the rule of the illustrious clan of Genghis Khan in China. The descendants of Kublai Khan became petty khans of the eastern lands of Mongolia and were often at war with each other.

The year 1370, when Toghon-Timur died, was a fateful

year for all the ruling houses of the descendants of Genghis Khan, in western Asia as well as in China. Hulagu's Persian empire had begun to collapse in 1335 under the rule of Abu-Said, and by 1370 it had disintegrated completely. The Golden Horde, ruled by descendants of Batu, also declined. The death in 1359 of Berdibeg, the tenth khan of the Golden Horde, marked the beginning of bitter struggle among pretenders to the throne, which lasted until 1370, when a new star rose over the empire created by Genghis Khan.

The name of the star was Timur-Bek, a Mongol but not a direct descendant of Genghis Khan. He was popularly known as Tamerlane.

5 From Tamerlane to Red Mongolia

The Mongol conquerors, from Genghis Khan to Tamerlane, very nearly succeeded in grasping the will-o'-the-wisp that has led so many conquerors to destruction—the conquest of the world. The Mongol empires of the thirteenth and fourteenth centuries came closer to becoming a common nation of all the peoples of the known world than the Roman Empire had. There was more movement of races and peoples during this period than at any other time in the history of mankind. First, there was the massive movement of Mongols from east to west, during which many nations and races added their blood to the peoples of the east. The Arabs, the Persians, the Armenians, the Slavs, and the Syrians and other Semitic peoples—all mixed and mingled with the Mongols and Tatars during the years of conquest. At the same time, thousands of Western peoples were uprooted and moved to Mongolia and China. During the Yuan Dynasty, there was a large military and agricultural colony of ten thousand Russians living in settlements near Peking. Thousands more Russians settled in Mongolia, and hundreds of thousands of Russians were sold in the slave markets of the Near East. Many of the famed Mamelukes, who ruled Egypt until the nineteenth century, were descendants of Russians sold into slavery by the Mongolian conquerors.

Tamerlane

In the last half of the fourteenth century, while eastern Mongolia was being torn by the squabbles of the petty khans, western Mongolia was coming under the rule of Timur, the last of the Mongolian conquerors to approach Genghis Khan in stature. Timur was born on April 9, 1336, into a princely but obscure Mongolian family that was not related to the descendants of Genghis Khan. Timur was once defeated in battle. Suffering from a leg wound, he disappeared into the desert until he had recovered and was able to avenge his defeat. When he reappeared, he was limping from the wound in his leg, which caused people to call him Timur the Lame, or Tamerlane.

In 1369, at the age of 33, after a series of successful but minor military campaigns in Central Asia, Tamerlane proclaimed himself ruler of all the lands lying between the Tien Shan and the Hindu Kush mountain ranges. Two years later, he completed his first major conquest, that of Khorezm in Central Asia, the ancient empire that had been subjugated by Genghis Khan 150 years before. Tamerlane not only destroyed the cities of Khorezm and slaughtered the inhabitants, but, like his predecessor, he destroyed the irrigation system as well. He then proceeded to Iran, whose many small princedoms required five years to subjugate. Wherever the hordes of Tamerlane went, they left utter devastation. Tamerlane's tactics differed from those of Genghis Khan, who had usually left behind him an efficient Mongol administration to retain effective control of the conquered people. Furthermore, the campaigns of Genghis Khan had been thorough. They were characterized by long periods of preparation, wise counsel, and a minimum of risk. Tamerlane favored lightning raids. He made decisions on the spur of the moment and often undertook risky and adventurous campaigns. He came, destroyed, and was gone. Those who were spared the sword were then free to return to what was left of their way of life. Since no strong Mongol administration was left behind, revolts were numerous. Tamerlane would return, and the revolt would be put down with blood-curdling effectiveness.

Early in his career, Tamerlane had befriended Tokhtamysh, who, with Tamerlane's assistance, became great khan of the Golden Horde in 1376. Tokhtamysh was ambitious beyond all bounds and was soon challenging Tamerlane for the leadership of all the Mongolian lands. In a series of campaigns, pitched battles, and political maneuvers, Tokhtamysh was temporarily defeated but managed to return from exile and resume his drive for power. His struggles with Tamerlane succeeded in slowing down and ultimately thwarting the latter's progress to the attainment of his ultimate goal, the conquest of the entire known world.

By 1388, Tamerlane had effectively occupied all of Persia, the Middle East, and Transcaucasia. Reaching the Volga River, he turned south toward the Don River, laid to waste the Crimea, and returned to the Caucasus. Iraq and the land of the Kurds were next. Baghdad was occupied in 1394, and the Euphrates River for a time became the western border of Tamerlane's possessions. The conqueror then swept into the empire of the Golden Horde, still held by Tokhtamysh, and destroyed the city of Saray at the mouth of the Volga. In

1398, he advanced on India, reached the Indus River, and captured Delhi, where he meted out the usual destruction. He then proceeded along the Ganges River. The Indian campaign was the bloodiest and most inhuman of all. When the vast army of prisoners Tamerlane had taken proved to be a liability to his army, he issued orders for their extermination, and 100,000 people were put to death.

The following year, Tamerlane was laying to waste the beautiful Georgian countryside in the Transcaucasian region. Orchards and vineyards were destroyed. The Georgians were massacred. While in Transcaucasia, Tamerlane learned that an alliance was being formed against him by the sultans of Baghdad and Egypt and by the Ottoman Turks. A sweeping raid ensued and carried him to the shores of the Mediterranean. The cities of Aleppo, Baalbek, and Damask suffered the complete destruction that had become the trademark of Tamerlane's conquests. Baghdad was destroyed next and its population exterminated. The extensive irrigation works around Baghdad were ruined, and the once flourishing state became a wasteland. To this day the Mesopotamian region has not completely recovered from the savage destruction wrought by Tamerlane.

The next campaign was directed against the empire of the Ottoman Turks. On July 1, 1402, the Turks were defeated in battle at Ankara, and the sultan was taken prisoner. Once more Tamerlane struck out along the Mediterranean coast, capturing the fortress of Smyrna, headquarters of the Knights of St. John. The Turks had stormed Smyrna many times, but always without success. Tamerlane accomplished the task without undue effort. The mere mention of his name was sufficient to instill terror in the hearts of the defenders. As retribution for their opposition, Tamerlane beheaded the captured knights and filled the boats that had been sent to their assistance with the heads of the knights and their followers.

Tamerlane was now almost 70 years old. Except for Western Europe and China, he had accomplished his dream of world conquest. He therefore returned to Samarkand to rest and make preparations for the reconquest of China. In January, 1405, he marched against China at the head of an enormous army, but by the time the Mongol hordes reached Otrar, Tamerlane was dead. The invasion was halted.

Tamerlane's conquests were in western Mongolia, Central Asia, Europe, and the Near East. He left untouched the less desirable lands belonging to the conglomeration of impoverished tribes in eastern Mongolia. When the huge empire Tamerlane had created from the bits and pieces of Genghis Khan's great empire was left without a leader, it quickly disintegrated into a multitude of states.

Tamerlane is remembered today not so much for his spectacular military exploits and conquests as for his cruelty, which far outstripped that of Genghis Khan. In addition to the 100,000-man massacre of Indian prisoners, the masterpieces of Tamerlane's cruelty include two incidents during his conquest of Persia: the construction of a tower made of two thousand living prisoners placed on top of each other and then covered with clay and broken brick and the burial alive of four thousand Moslem prisoners.

From Tamerlane to the Twentieth Century

After the death of Tamerlane, the Mongols played a secondary role in the history of Asia. For many years, various influences had been at work and eventually divided the Mongols into two distinct branches—the Oirats of western Mongolia and the Khalkha Mongols of eastern Mongolia. After Tamerlane, the destiny of the western Mongols was to be linked with that of Central Asia (Sinkiang, Turkistan, and Afghanistan). The majority of the Mongols in the present Mongolian People's Republic are descendants of the Khalkha Mongols. Since these are the people that we are to deal with in the remainder of this book, it is their story that most concerns us here.

Eastern Mongolia retained its independent status for nearly 250 years after the collapse of the Yuan Dynasty in 1370, but the area was in a sorry state. Petty struggles among princely houses, palace assassinations, raids against neighbors, and an almost constant changing of khans were commonplace, as were the struggles for the title of great khan, who, nevertheless, seldom was able to exercise any real political power.

Only once during these years was the country unified under the leadership of a competent great khan. Dayan Khan ruled during the first half of the fifteenth century. After his death, eastern Mongolia was again torn by internal strife. The last great khan to attempt to force his will on other khans and princes was Ligdan Khan of Chahar, who reigned at the beginning of the seventeenth century. He met with little success. By that time, a tribe of people, the Manchus, centered in Manchuria, east of Mongolia, had begun to threaten Mongolia and to challenge the authority of the Ming Dynasty in China. In an incredibly short time, the Manchus emerged from the plains of Manchuria into the fertile valleys of China, which was still ruled by the weak emperors of the Ming Dynasty. The westward pressure exerted by the Manchus proved too strong for Ligdan Khan, who abandoned the Mongol princes in eastern Mongolia. Unable to obtain support from the Mongol princes in the west, he retreated to the shores of Koko Nur in Central Asia, where he died in 1634. Two years later, the Manchus formally annexed southern Mongolia. They entered Peking in 1644 and established the Ch'ing Dynasty, which was to last until 1911. However, they were not able to extend their rule to northern Mongolia until 1691.

The piecemeal conquest of Mongolia had the effect of dividing the country politically into north and south, a division that persists. Southern Mongolia is now the Inner Mongolian Autonomous Region of China (Inner Mongolia). Northern Mongolia is the independent Mongolian People's Republic (sometimes referred to as Outer Mongolia but more often merely as Mongolia).

After eastern Mongolia had been subjugated by the Manchus, it was in danger of conquest by the Oirats of western Mongolia, but they were defeated by the Manchus and were made part of the Chinese Empire in 1758. Today the land of the Oirats is part of the Sinkiang-Uighur Autonomous Region of China.

Outer Mongolia was ruled by China until the collapse of the Ch'ing Dynasty in 1911, when, somewhat prematurely, the country declared its independence.

The Birth of Red Mongolia

Mongolia's newly found independence lasted until 1915, when it was forced to recognize the suzerainty of the Chinese government as a result of a tripartite agreement concluded with China and Russia. According to the treaty, Mongolia was to remain inside the borders of the Chinese Republic but was to be fully autonomous.

With the outbreak of the Russian Revolution in 1917 and the civil war that raged in Siberia and the Russian Far East for the next five years, Mongolia became a pawn in the struggle between the White and Red Russian armies. In March, 1918, the Chinese took advantage of the unsettled situation and the general collapse of Russian authority in Siberia and sent troops to occupy Urga, then capital of Mongolia. This was a violation of the treaty of 1915, but the Russians were in no position to either protest the violation or help Mongolia resist the invasion. The Peking government had ambitious plans for Mongolia. In October, 1919, General Hsu Shu-cheng, known as "Little Hsu," assumed firm control of Mongolia. Within a month, the Chinese government had repudiated the 1915 treaty and had declared Mongolia an integral part of China.

The following year was crucial in the struggle between the warring Russian armies. The White army in the vicinity of Mongolia was hard pressed by the Red army. Baron Ungern von Sternberg, commander of a White Russian cavalry detachment, crossed the Mongolian border with his troops and reached Urga in October, 1920. He was repulsed by the Chinese troops and retreated, but not before he had announced to all the world that he was destined to save Asia and possibly Europe from the Red peril, although, in his opinion, Europe was hardly worth saving. He was determined to form a new, great Mongolian nation with himself as leader.

Baron Ungern was considered an able military officer. A

natural leader, he had distinguished himself in the Russo-Japanese War of 1904–5. He had served a tour of duty in Mongolia in 1910 as an officer of the Russian imperial army, guarding the Russian consulate in Urga and had been decorated for bravery in World War I. However, the Baron's actions in 1920 and for the next several months indicated that he was mentally unbalanced, perhaps because of the horrible death his family had met at the hands of the Bolsheviks. At any rate, he made known his plans for eliminating Communism and restoring monarchy in Russia, China, and Mongolia. He would liquidate all Communists so unfortunate as to fall into his hands.

Undaunted by his failure to capture Urga in October, Baron Ungern attacked again and entered the city on February 3, 1921. The Chinese retreated in disorder. Red sympathizers, particularly Jews, were rounded up by the Baron's troops and summarily executed. Nevertheless, Ungern was popular with the Mongols. His aspirations for Mongolia and his avowed intention of retaining Bodgo Gegen, the Lamaist monarch, as religious leader appealed to them, and his original White army force of 800 men was soon augmented by 10,000 Mongolian volunteers.

While Ungern made plans for carrying out his wild designs, an event of great importance to the future of Mongolia was occurring in the town of Troitskosavsk on the Russian side of the border. A small group of Mongols, gathered there under the protection of the Red army bayonets, was forming a new Mongolian People's Government. The Mongolian revolutionary leader Sukhe Bator was elected war minister of the new government and commander-in-chief of the tiny Mongolian revolutionary army.

There followed an amazing episode, half farce, half tragedy. Ungern had decided not only to defend Mongolia against its Communist neighbor to the north but also to invade Russia and liberate the Russian people. He made an abortive attack on Troitskosavsk on May 22, 1921. The newly formed army of Sukhe Bator was no match for the disciplined forces of the Baron, but the Red army detachments were able to force Ungern and his men back into Mongolia. Sukhe Bator then begged the Soviet command to help him expel Ungern, and the Red army pursued Ungern and his troops across the border. Many of the Mongols in Ungern's army deserted, and some dissatisfied Russians, suspecting that the Baron was mad, followed their example. The Red army units entered Urga on July 8, and two days later the new Mongolian government was installed, with Sukhe Bator as war minister and commander-in-chief. His assistant Choibalsan became his deputy.

Ungern was not ready to give up. He escaped the pursuing Red forces and fled with a small group of supporters. On August 22, an attempt was made on his life, but he was able to ride to safety and reached the Mongolian unit under his command. However, the unit by this time had decided that it had had enough and handed Ungern over to the Red army. On September 15, 1921, Baron Ungern von Sternberg was found guilty of crimes against the Soviet state by a court-martial in Siberia and was executed.

The first act of the new Mongolian People's Government was to declare its independence on July 11, 1921. It was a qualified independence, however, heavily oriented toward Russia because of the explosive international situation existing in the Far East. In spite of internal struggles among its own warlords, China was casting covetous glances at Mongolia, and only the presence of the Soviet army prevented the Chinese from attempting to recover its lost satellite. Japan, at that time the most powerful political and military force in the Orient, also posed a threat. In order to preserve its precarious independence, Mongolia found it necessary to accept Russian support.

The new country cooperated with the Soviet Union from the beginning. An agreement of friendship and mutual assistance was signed on November 5, 1921. One of the surprising features of the early years of the newly independent state was that the Communist leaders permitted the Mongols to retain the religious leader Bogdo Gegen as nominal head of state. Secular power, however, was vested in Sukhe Bator, who was succeeded by Choibalsan.

The country was declared a republic in 1924, upon the death of Bogdo Gegen. Supreme power was entrusted to the *Khural* (People's Parliament), modeled after Russia's ruling body, the Supreme Soviet. A new constitution was adopted on November 24, 1925, and the name of the capital was changed from Urga to Ulan Bator. The Mongolian People's Republic thus became a Soviet satellite in form as well as in fact. Under Choibalsan, Stalin's gradual introduction of the use of terror to control the agricultural sector of the Russian economy and its later use against the population in general were slavishly copied by Mongol party leaders. Many party comrades of Choibalsan, some of whom had participated in building the new Mongolian state, were liquidated. The same fate befell landowners and priests, who were eliminated as classes in the years 1929–31. Livestock and property were officially distributed to the poorer peasants but actually became the property of the state. Temples and monasteries were closed. Lamas (Lamaist monks) who were not executed were forced into secular activities, although the choice of such activities was extremely limited. The policy of confiscation, which affected not only lamas and landowners but also well-to-do peasants, led to the massive Lama Rebellion of 1932, so called because of the discontented lamas who led thousands of people across the border into voluntary exile in Inner Mongolia, taking their livestock with them. According to official Soviet statistics, the Lama Rebellion diminished the livestock population of Monoglia by 7 million head.

Because of the Lama Rebellion, many thousands of active party members were accused of deviation and were purged. Left deviationists were accused of perverting the party line by actively persecuting priests and taking over monasteries instead of coming to grips with the feudal, theocratic upper layers of Lamaism. Right deviationists were accused of attempting to restore capitalism and impose a feudal regime on the country.

Mongol-Soviet cooperation continued unabated during these trying years. Large quantities of materials were poured into the country; financial assistance was not lacking. A second Soviet-Mongolian Treaty of Mutual Assistance was signed in Ulan Bator on March 12, 1936, and was honored by Russia when the Japanese Kwantung army of Manchuria attempted to invade eastern Mongolia in May, 1939. The Mongols, aided by Russian troops, planes, and tanks, succeeded in routing several Japanese divisions, which had hoped to colonize Mongolia as they had Manchuria—which was then the so-called independent state of Manchukuo, ruled by the Emperor Kang-Teh but actually governed by Japanese advisers.

When Russia was invaded by Germany during World War II, Mongolia abstained from actively participating in the war but supplied food, cattle, and horses to its hardpressed neighbor. Mongolia's active participation in the war did not occur until a few days before Japan's surrender in August, 1945, when the Russians invaded Manchuria with the aid of Mongolian military units, largely cavalry. The Mongol horsemen crossed the Gobi Desert and invaded enemy-held areas in north China, far in the rear of the Japanese army.

October 20, 1945, was a milestone in the history of Mongolia. Up until this day, Nationalist China had stubbornly refused to recognize Mongolian independence. Stalin, earlier in 1945, at the Yalta Conference, had agreed to participate in the war against Japan only on the condition that a plebiscite be held in Mongolia to decide whether the country wished to become fully independent or to be included as an autonomous region within the Chinese state. All 487,409 Mongols taking part in the plebiscite (98.4 per cent of the adult population) voted for independence. Nationalist China had to bow to this popular decision.

For many years, Mongolia was denied membership in the United Nations, but a "package deal" was finally made between the democratic world and the Communist bloc. The Soviet Union agreed not to oppose the admission of Mauritania if the democratic countries would abstain from opposing the admission of Mongolia. Mongolia thus became a full-fledged member of the United Nations in October, 1961.

6 Painful Growth

In many ways the history of independent Mongolia resembles that of the Soviet Union, its neighbor to the north. The country has had its share of purges and bloodshed since 1911, but it has not had a dearth of leaders. Many prominent men have contributed to the creation and existence of the new state. Not all of them can be said to have been successful, however, and only three managed to stay on top for any length of time. The others failed in one important respect: to stay alive. The three leaders who survived long enough to leave their mark upon the country were Sukhe Bator, Choibalsan, and Tsedenbal.

The first two leaders engraved their names on the pages of the early history of the Mongolian People's Republic. In 1919, two small revolutionary groups of Mongols were formed independently of each other—one under the leadership of Sukhe Bator and the other under the leadership of Choibalsan. The two leaders had never met. A reason for the emergence of these two particular men was that they were both literate in a country that, except for the priestly lamas, was almost wholly illiterate. Both had received some education in their younger days, and both had mastered Russian

—the foreign language that was to stand them in good stead in their future careers.

Sukhe Bator, like Choibalsan, had been born into a poor family. At the age of 14, he was able to get a job as a mail rider and courier. Although the job was not pleasant, it placed him in contact with educated Mongols, and he was able to pick up the beginning of his education. The Chinese revolution of 1911 provided the second stage of his education. Outer Mongolia at that time became an autonomous state, though only temporarily, and Sukhe Bator was conscripted into the national Mongolian army, which consisted of illiterate country youths. Because of his smattering of education and the fact that he could read and write, Sukhe Bator was soon promoted and became a noncommissioned officer.

Sukhe Bator was not of noble blood, and in normal times he would have spent his lifetime in the noncommissioned ranks of the army. But times were far from normal. After the Russian Revolution began, the Chinese took advantage of the civil war raging in the Siberian countryside and moved into Urga, the capital of Mongolia. The national Mongolian army was promptly disbanded, and in 1919, along with thousands of other men, Sukhe Bator found himself an ex-soldier. Most of the former soldiers, uprooted from their familiar nomadic way of life, had experienced in the army a different kind of existence from that of their fathers. They found themselves alienated from their homes. Under these conditions, 26-year-old Sukhe Bator did not find it hard to gather around him a band of ex-soldiers and to assume leadership.

The excesses being committed at that time by Baron Ungern von Sternberg were instrumental in molding Sukhe

Bator's thinking. His reaction to such excesses pushed the young leader to the fore in the Mongolian revolutionary movement. His motivation was not Marxist; he knew little of the ideology that had sparked the struggle in Russia. Indeed, he was quite naive when it came to politics, being more of a nationalist than a Marxist or internationalist.

In contrast to Sukhe Bator, Choibalsan was a dedicated Marxist. He had received some formal education, was well read, and had been in contact with Russian revolutionaries in Siberia even before the Revolution. His youth had been spent in a monastery, which he had entered at the age of 13. When he was 17, he ran away to Urga and entered a school for interpreters. Apparently, he was proficient in his studies, for he was soon sent to Irkutsk in eastern Siberia to study in the Russian high school there. With the coming of the Russian Revolution, he was forced to leave Irkutsk and return to Mongolia where, in 1919, quite independently of Sukhe Bator, he organized a revolutionary group. He was 24 years old at the time. His followers, unlike the ex-soldiers led by Sukhe Bator, were dissatisfied members of the civilian segment of Mongolian society.

Both Choibalsan and Sukhe Bator counted among their followers members of the only two literate classes in the country—the lamas and former officials of autonomous Outer Mongolia—many of whom probably were more able and politically experienced than either of the two young leaders. They also attracted an exceptionally able leader, Maksarjab, who had become known in 1911 at the time of the Chinese revolution when he fought against the Manchu overlords of Mongolia. Later he joined forces with Baron Ungern for purely nationalistic reasons: to aid the Baron to drive the

Chinese out of Urga. For a while, Maksarjab was minister of war in the government set up by Ungern. When it became apparent that Ungern's primary motivation was not the independence of the Mongols, Maksarjab joined forces with Sukhe Bator and Choibalsan, but like many of the early Mongol revolutionaries, he eventually turned against the two successful leaders, was declared a traitor, and lost his life.

Sukhe Bator and Choibalsan did not come face to face until 1921, when the leaders and delegates of both revolutionary groups assembled in the Siberian town of Kyakhta, just across the border from Mongolia. Baron Ungern von Sternberg was still powerful in Mongolia, and the fact that it was necessary to convene this historical group on Russian soil is a clear indication of how little support the revolutionary movement had in Mongolia. Nevertheless, on March 1, 1921, the twenty-six delegates to the meeting brought into being a new political party—the Mongolian People's Revolutionary party, which has survived to this day.

The twenty-six delegates to the Kyakhta congress were able to muster about four hundred warriors. Having decided to invade Mongolia, they crossed the border with this small but loyal force and occupied the town of Maimachen and formed a new national government. The new government's meager resources and almost complete lack of popular support would have spelled doom for the leaders and the entire force if the Soviet Union had not stepped in and rendered assistance. It is perhaps more accurate to say that the revolutionaries invited the Red army into Mongolia. In any event, the augmented forces swiftly moved on Urga, put an end to the rule of Baron Ungern, and installed the small band of

Mongol revolutionaries as the official government of independent Mongolia. From such comic-opera beginnings did the new nation come into existence. The assistance of Russian troops had more or less guaranteed that the nation would be similar to and dominated by the Soviet Union. For the first few years, the new nation led a precarious existence. The coalition government formed by the original small band of revolutionaries included among its officials many former nobles and lamas. Bogdo Gegen, the "Living Buddha," was retained as the religious and nominal secular head of state. Secular power was really vested in a cabinet of ministers under the premiership of a former lama named Bodo. A close associate of Bogdo Gegen, Bodo had been one of the first lamas to join the group of revolutionaries organized by Sukhe Bator.

For over a year, the helm of the new government was in the hands of Bodo, with Sukhe Bator holding the posts of war minister and commander-in-chief of the armed forces. The nationalistic trends of the fledgling government, however, did not suit the aims of the Soviet Union, which had assumed that the early 1920's would see general uprisings and the collapse of governments throughout the entire world. To combat the nationalistic trend in Mongolia, Soviet state security agents were sent into the country. The results soon became evident. Bodo and fourteen other leaders of the administration were arrested and tried on trumped-up charges. Among the accusations made was that of being pro-Chinese. On August 30, 1922, this group of "traitors" was shot. Most of the fifteen executed leaders had been with the twenty-six men present at the birth of the new nation at Kyakhta only one year before. From the time of the execu-

This woman and her children are among the slightly more than a million citizens of Mongolia. In a country where the population density is less than two per square mile, state medals are awarded the mothers of large families.

Much in Mongolia is changing . . . much remains the same. Here, herdsmen buy goods from a state store that travels the countryside in the same way as private peddlers did for centuries.

A troupe of actors entertains the inhabitants of traditional felt yurts in this remote camp (above), but other Mongolians today live in apartment buildings, like these in the new town of Nalaikha (below), and earn their living as miners and industrial workers.

A team of government tractors breaking virgin land for a new state farm (above), tank cars on the Trans-Mongolian Railroad (right), and the new oil refinery at Dzun-Bayn (below) all attest to Mongolia's efforts at modernization.

Livestock remains the basic source of wealth. Wool from hardy Mongolian sheep like these is the country's major export.

Enormous timber reserves are a promising source of future growth. The timber in this spring log jam will be rafted downriver to one of Mongolia's new lumber mills. But better transportation must be built before large-scale lumbering can develop.

COMECON assistance has been a major spur to Mongolia's industry. Above, a Soviet technical adviser inspects a power substation. Below, workers in Darkhan's textile mill (equipped with Czech and East German machinery) are instructed by their foreman.

A steamer plies the calm waters of Lake Khopsogol en route to the Soviet Union.

A new generation listens to a lecture at the Mongolian State University, which was established at Ulan Bator in 1942.

Diversity and continuity are reflected in these recent theatrical productions by the State Theater of Opera and Ballet:

performances of the Russian opera *Rusalka*, by Dargomizhsky;

Three Sad Hills, a modern opera based on Mongolian folk themes;

and *Otello*, translated into Mongolian.

The home of Sukhe Bator, Mongolia's revolutionary leader, is now a state museum in Ulan Bator.

The lake region of western Mongolia presents an enchanting contrast to the rock-strewn, arid Gobi region of the southeast.

tion until the present, the pattern of events in Mongolia has followed the pattern of events in the Soviet Union.

The following year, 1923, Sukhe Bator died. Although it was widely known that he had succumbed to tuberculosis, it was officially stated that he had been poisoned by lamas. This charge boded ill for the lamas. Sukhe Bator became, in death, a national hero, and his name became surrounded with the aura of the savior of his country, whereas if he had lived for a few more years, it is quite possible that he would have fallen victim to his rival, the scheming and ruthless Choibalsan. A year later, in 1924, Bodgo Gegen died. All pretense of a coalition government of divergent political groups and classes was abandoned. The country became a Soviet-style nation and assumed its present name, Mongolian People's Republic, in June, 1924.

After the death of Sukhe Bator, purges and executions became the order of the day. The able but ambitious Danzan assumed the duties of vice-premier and commander-in-chief of the army, but before the year was out Danzan and his aide Bavasan had been arrested after a stormy session of the Third Congress of the Mongolian People's Revolutionary Party. Both Danzan and Bavasan were shot. Their execution was traced to Rinchino, one of the two Buryats from eastern Siberia who had been among the twenty-six delegates present at the original congress in Kyakhta (the other was Zhamtsarano). Rinchino was an official delegate from the Soviet Comintern; his job was to keep an eye on the new revolutionary party and its leaders. His victory over Danzan and Bavasan was short lived. In 1925, he was removed from his post as Comintern representative and was soon sent back to Russia, where he lived until the wave of Russian purges caught up with him. He was executed in 1937. Zhamtsarano was sent to Leningrad in 1932 and was arrested in 1937, the same year that Rinchino was shot, after which there is no trace of him. He probably died in a concentration camp.

The elimination of Danzan and Bavasan paved the way for Choibalsan, who became commander-in-chief of the army after Danzan's execution. Rung by rung, he began his climb up the ladder to absolute power in much the same way that Stalin was making his way to the top in Russia. One of the results of Choibalsan's elevation was the wave of purges that struck Mongolia in 1928 when Damba Dorji, chairman of the central committee of the party, was accused of rightist leanings and was exiled to Moscow, where he died in 1932. His numerous followers were removed from office or purged as "right deviationists."

During the next decade there was an orgy of purges and executions. The lists of persons sentenced to death by shooting, published in official Mongolian newspapers at the time, included prime ministers, high lamas, truck drivers, and ordinary herdsmen. In 1930 and 1931, of the more than eight hundred households expropriated by the state, two hundred belonged to ecclesiastical officials, almost all of whom had either been shot or imprisoned. The second major purge occurred in 1932, when "left deviationists" were accused of excessively rapid and disastrous collectivization. The result was the appalling, willful destruction of Mongolia's most precious commodity—its livestock (see Chapter 10).

As Choibalsan rose to power, attacks on the church, on the remnants of the nobility, on merchants, on well-to-do peasants, and on Choibalsan's political adversaries increased in savagery. In 1937 and 1938 alone, two thousand lamas whose crime was holding ecclesiastical positions were shot. By the end of the 1930's, the lamas and the aristocracy had been eliminated as a class. Not all the nobles and lamas were put to death; some escaped to Inner Mongolia, where they settled among their Mongol relatives.

The purges affected every level of Mongol society. The executions made inroads into the ranks of the government, the Comintern, the central committee of the party, and into that most sacrosanct group of all—the party secretariat. In 1932, the Mongolian People's Revolutionary Party boasted forty-two thousand members. Two years later, about eight thousand remained. The Communist youth organization, Revsomol, was not spared. Practically all its leaders were purged, shot, or imprisoned, and the organization was dissolved in 1934. When it was re-established in 1935, its registered membership was slightly over six thousand, as compared to twenty-three thousand before it was disbanded. The bloody hand of the executioner did not spare the army. At about the same time that Marshal Tukhachevsky was being sentenced to death in Russia under Stalin, Choibalsan's security forces were making accusations against Marshal Demid, commander-in-chief of the Mongolian army. Demid was not shot. He was put aboard a train for Moscow in 1937 and died of "poisoning" on the way.

In the meantime, Choibalsan, emulating Stalin, continued his uninterrupted climb to the top. In 1937, in his role as minister of the interior and with the security forces under his command, he succeeded in liquidating Prime Minister Gendun. Two years later, Gendun's popular successor, Amor, was executed, together with several other high officials, and Choibalsan himself became prime minister. By the end of the decade he had reached the pinnacle. His rivals had been eliminated. He was the only surviving member of the original Kyakhta group of twenty-six.

The next decade (1941–50), which paralleled the years of Stalin's glory in Russia, saw the rise of a "personality cult" in Mongolia, which took the form of an excessive adulation of Choibalsan. Then, on January 28, 1952, slightly more than a year before the death of Stalin, Choibalsan died of cancer in a Moscow hospital. With his demise a new era began in Mongolian political life. The succeeding government was more liberal and less awe-inspiring than the old. It was still ruled by the will of one man, but the new leader was not a military figure. He was a technocrat (a bureaucrat with technical training) by the name of Tsedenbal.

Tsedenbal had been 5 years old when the rag bag army of Sukhe Bator began its invasion of Mongolia in 1921. By the time Tsedenbal came of age in the early 1930's, the Buryats, who had been particularly strong in the 1920's, had ceased to be a political force in Mongolia, and the influence of the Khalkha Mongols, who represented 90 per cent of the entire population, had become powerful. The elimination of the Buryats from the political scene played into the hands of the young Khalkha Mongol Tsedenbal. In 1940, at the age of 24, he became secretary of the central committee of the party, under the tutelage of Choibalsan. Although few knew it at the time, a new star had appeared on the political horizon.

The fact that a young politician like Tsedenbal, rather than an old-line revolutionary, took over the government is significant. It marked a change in the power structure of Mongolia. Old party members who had participated in the revolution of 1921 and in the formation of the new social structure were forced to hand over the reins of government to those who had been born after the revolution or who had been children during the time of the social upheavals of the 1920's.

It was high time. Fratricidal struggles among the original revolutionaries had decimated their ranks. Those who remained were dying out, making room for the younger generation, which was the product of training received in the Communist youth organization. The new generation was not a military one. Its members could boast no spectacular military victories and had not taken part in revolutionary struggles. Some had received military ranks during World War II, but not for valor or for excellence in military operations. Mongolia had not entered the conflict until the last few days of the war, when, as an ally of the Soviet Union, it had taken part in the blitzkrieg against Japanese forces in China. Military rank in the Mongolian army was a sign more of political than military success. Tsedenbal, for example, had been a lieutenant-general as deputy commander-in-chief of the armed forces, but his position was actually that of political overseer, with a secondary title of director of political indoctrination.

Essentially, the new politicians were civilians. They were well-educated, well-trained specialists—which could not have been said of the early revolutionary leaders, most of whom had not had any formal education. Tsedenbal had specialized in economics. He had been an instructor in the School of Economics in Ulan Bator until 1939. Like the majority of the leaders of his generation, he was a technocrat.

Taking over the government of the Mongolian state was not a simple matter. When Choibalsan died, Tsedenbal became prime minister, but a tug-of-war immediately set in behind the scenes. It resulted in a temporary loss of power for Tsedenbal. His job as secretary of the central committee of the party was given to Damba. For four years the two men ruled behind a façade of unity. By 1958, Tsedenbal had gathered enough influential supporters to remove Damba under the pretext that he was pro-Chinese. Tsedenbal then resumed his position as secretary of the central committee and became head of both party and government, the undisputed master of Mongolia.

Holding a dual post has not been easy, because liberalizing tendencies have been permeating practically all the Communist nations, except for China and perhaps Albania. Tsedenbal has had to exert every means to maintain his position and preserve control of the state. The first necessity was to remove Choibalsan's supporters from high positions in the government and party. This he accomplished by a series of purges in 1962 and 1963. The new policy, called "de-Choibalsanization," consisted of accusing the former aides of the dead leader of promoting a personality cult. In this way Tsedenbal was able to remove some of his most dangerous and potentially dangerous rivals, including the minister of public security and head of the secret police—the most feared man in Mongolia. The director of the army's political section was also removed, together with the army chief of staff and the commander of the garrison forces in Ulan Bator. With the security forces and the army under control, Tsedenbal moved against the number two leader of the politburo—L. Tsende, second secretary of the central committee. Tsende was purged in December, 1963. From that time to the present, Tsedenbal has appeared to be in complete control of the government of Mongolia and of its military and political parts. To Tsedenbal's credit, it should be said that there have been no executions in his purges. He seems to have taken his cue from Khrushchev, who sent old-time revolutionaries like Molotov and Kaganovich into exile.

The road to progress of formerly backward and illiterate Mongolia has been bloody. Thousands have been sacrificed, and one of the ironies of this sacrifice is that many of those who perished were not opponents of the new order but those who had helped to create the new state. However, indications are that the bloodbath of the 1920's, 1930's, and 1940's will not be repeated. Mongolian society is still totalitarian, but changes are taking place.

7 The Government

Several changes in the administrative divisions of Mongolia have been made since the end of the seventeenth century, when the country was first ruled by the Manchu Dynasty of China. At one time, the entire area of what is now the Mongolian People's Republic was divided into four large *aymags* (provinces), to which must be added the Kobdo region to the west, which was occupied by the Oirats, who were politically united with the Mongols. This five-part administrative structure was unwieldly, and the country was later subdivided in 111 hereditary dukedoms, which existed until 1911.

The present Communist rulers have divided the country into eighteen *aymags* on the basis of geographical boundaries, economic conditions, ethnic differences, population distribution, and convenience of administrative control. *Aymags* vary in size from 63,700 to 16,600 square miles. Each *aymag* is divided into from twelve to twenty-six *somons,* which correspond to U.S. counties, and each *aymag* has at least one *khoron* (municipal administrative district). Ulan Bator is divided into eleven *khorons*. The only large city in Mongolia, it has a population of more than 200,000. Administratively, it is not part of any of the eighteen *aymags* but is administered independently, like the capital of the United States in the District of Columbia.

Former Soviet Premier Khrushchev once pointed out that at the end of World War II in 1945 only two countries in the world had Communist systems of government—the Soviet Union and the Mongolian People's Republic. The evolution of Communist rule in Mongolia was similar to its evolution in the Soviet Union, with forced collectivization of peasants, confiscation of private property, and dreadful purges. As a consequence, the composition of the present Mongolian government is like that of the Soviet Union. The *Khural* (Supreme Council) elects a presidium to administer the country between sessions of the *Khural*. The constitution of Mongolia is similar to that of the Soviet Union. The legislative, executive, and judicial branches of the government differ only in name from those of the Soviets.

Present government authority is derived from the constitution of 1960, which provides for the election every three years of the *Khural,* the highest administrative body in the state. Every able-bodied citizen is required to participate in the election, although the bloc of candidates elected has usually been selected well in advance by the party organization. In the 1960 elections, for instance, 99.98 per cent of the voters voted for the official candidates. Of the 267 candidates elected to the *Khural* at that time, slightly more than 40 per cent were white-collar workers, approximately 33 per cent were representatives of the collectivized agricultural communities, and about 25 per cent represented industrial and other types of workers.

Members of the *Khural* meet briefly once a year in the

capital. If an emergency arises between sessions, they can be recalled upon demand by one-third of the members or by the presidium, which rules the country between sessions. The presidium consists of a chairman, a deputy chairman, a secretary, and six members of the *Khural*.

The highest executive body of the state is the council of ministers, selected by the *Khural* at its annual session. Judicial power is vested in a supreme court, assisted by *aymag* courts (similar to U.S. district courts), municipal courts, and special courts. Members of the supreme court are appointed for three-year terms by the *Khural,* as is the procurator general, whose role is like that of the U.S. attorney general.

None of these officials or official bodies, however, is the true ruler of Mongolia. Behind all official proclamations, decrees, and functions stands the all-powerful Mongolian People's Revolutionary party, the country's one and only political party.

Except for occasional isolated and unsuccessful attempts at rebellion, organized political activity was virtually nonexistent in Mongolia during the rule of the Manchu Dynasty. Not until the Communists took over in 1921 did a Mongolian political party come into being. In March of that year, Sukhe Bator and Choibalsan called a conference at the town of Kyakhta on the Russian border, and the Mongolian People's Revolutionary party was born. The party was installed at the head of the new independent state with the military assistance of the Soviet Union, and Lenin hastened to recognize the new government and establish diplomatic relations. Mongolia's first international agreement was signed with the government of the Soviet Union on November 5, 1921.

The change-over from an almost feudal system to a Communist form of government was gradual. War-torn Mongolia had suffered not only under the Chinese but also when the small but efficient mobile force of White Russian cavalry led by Baron Ungern von Sternberg expelled the Chinese and had in turn been defeated by Ungern's Russian rivals. It is doubtful that Sukhe Bator and his followers could have attained the power they did had they not acted cautiously. Realizing the strong hold the Lamaist religion—a Mongolian-Tibetan variety of Buddhism—had on the people of Mongolia, they allowed Bodgo Gegen, the monarch as well as the supreme head of the church, to retain his throne but limited his power to strictly religious affairs. Secular power was vested in Premier Bodo and in Sukhe Bator, who was both war minister and commander-in-chief of the army until his death in 1923. Among other reasons for this unusual marriage of Communism and religion was the very complicated international situation, for both China and Japan were jealously watching the changes taking place in Mongolia with the assistance and encouragement of the Soviet Union.

This precarious state of affairs lasted until 1924, when Bodgo Gegen died and the Communist rulers of the country decided that the time had come for a complete takeover. Princes and landlords were liquidated, and their property and livestock were confiscated by the state, as had been done in the Soviet Union. The Communists acted warily, however, and, while they proceeded energetically to wipe out every vestige of the old aristocracy, they were careful not to step on the toes of the religious leaders. After three years of Communist domination, the Lamaist religion was still extremely influential throughout Mongolia. With the death of Sukhe Bator, leadership fell to the ambitious Choibalsan, whose actions and behavior strongly resembled those of the Soviet dictator Stalin. Like Stalin, Choibalsan was denounced a few years after his death in 1952, for having introduced a personality cult into Mongolia. Typical of these denunciations were the words of the secretary of the Mongolian Writers' Union at the Union's 1962 congress: "The dangerous consequence of the personality cult instituted in the Choibalsan era was the use of literature to distort history and the party's role in it and its use as a weapon for the promotion of the personality cult. Literature could exist under Choibalsan only if it was willing to sing his praises and to exaggerate his part in our country's progress."

The Mongolian People's Revolutionary party experienced internal struggles similar to those of the Communist Party of the Soviet Union under Stalin. The first major split in the party occurred in 1928, when the "right deviationists" suffered the same fate as Stalin's opponents in Russia. The "left deviationists" were liquidated in 1932. The left wing was blamed for all the mistakes the party had made: for not taking into consideration the traditional way of life in Mongolia, for trying to collectivize a population still largely nomadic, and for generally upsetting the economic life of the country—all echoes of accusations and self-accusations made in purges in Soviet Russia itself.

What proportion of the total population of Mongolia is represented in the political party that rules the nation? About 5 per cent of the people either are members of the Mongolian People's Revolutionary party or are candidates for membership, roughly the same percentage as in the Soviet Union. Members and candidates for membership at the time of the fifteenth congress of the party in June, 1966, totaled 48,570. Of these, about 50 per cent were white-collar workers; a little more than 20 per cent were agricultural workers; and slightly less than 30 per cent were industrial and other workers. Of all party members and candidates, 20 per cent were women. The central committee of the party in 1966 consisted of seventy-five members and fifty-one candidates for membership, while the politburo consisted of seven members, headed by Yumzhaghiyuin Tsedenbal, first secretary of the central committee and Choibalsan's successor.

The government structure of the Mongolian People's Republic is similar to that of other states in the Communist orbit. All high officials of the state belong to the Mongolian People's Revolutionary party. The party's word is law, and the party is the ruler of the country.

8 The Economy

Fifty years ago, Mongolia had just thrown off Chinese rule. The nation had scarcely any industry and agriculture. Herding livestock represented the country's only significant economic activity. To be sure, a few industries and some trade—mostly foreign—had existed in the pre-Communist era in Urga, the sleepy little capital of Mongolia. Import-export firms exported furs, hides, and other raw materials and imported finished products, mainly textiles and items for household use. But practically every transaction with a foreign country was conducted by foreign merchants, most of whom were Russian. There was also a sprinkling of American, British, and German firms. What domestic trade existed was firmly in the hands of small Chinese business establishments. Urga had only a few thousand inhabitants, and other Mongolian towns were not much larger than outpost settlements. The percentage of the urban population engaged in typical small-town occupations was very small indeed. The outside world's impression of Mongolia as a vast prairie, with a few nomadic herdsmen scattered about, a few mountain ranges in the north and west, and the Gobi Desert in the south, was substantially correct.

Several factors had hindered the economic growth of Mongolia. The peasants lived in a semifeudal relationship with the landowners. The huge class of lamas, living a priestly but unproductive existence in lamaist monasteries, but who nevertheless owned a large percentage of Mongolia's livestock, was a drag on the economic life of the country. The products of animal husbandry accounted for almost 90 per cent of the national economy, and even products destined for export, mainly to China and Russia (and to a lesser extent England and the United States), were raw and unprocessed. Transport was by pack animals, who leisurely picked their way along paths that had been trodden since the days of Genghis Khan. Modern types of transportation (such as horse-drawn carts) were seen only occasionally. There were no roads except those connecting such well-developed settlements as Urga, Ulyassutai, and Kobdo with Kyakhta on the Russian border and Kalgan in China.

The picture has drastically changed. Mongolia now has a well-developed economy, which, in spite of many new factories and plants, coal mines, railroads, highways, and electric power facilities, is heavily oriented toward animal husbandry and its products and, to some extent, toward agriculture. However, the tempo of industrial growth during the last fifty years has been much greater than that of agriculture. During the 1930's, an attempt was made to diversify the country's economy. New factories and plants were constructed with Soviet help. Railroad construction was inaugurated in the early 1940's, and in 1948 Mongolia embarked on the first of a series of five-year plans.

Although the first five-year plan (1948–52) was aimed at increasing overall economic development and the maximum utilization of natural resources, the main effort was devoted to the improvement of animal husbandry. The second five-year plan (1953–57), which made additional changes in the economic picture, also caused rapid gains in the development of industry, and there was a simultaneous increase in agricultural production. As in most countries in which the largest part of the population is engaged in nomadic cattle-raising and horse-raising, agriculture had remained a minor economic activity. Under the second five-year plan large areas were consigned to the plow. Another period of planned economy followed; the three-year plan of 1958–60 concentrated on developing all parts of the economy.

During these periods of planned economic development, the rate and value of capital investment increased rapidly, from 203.7 million *tugriks* during the first five-year plan to almost 600 million during the second five-year plan, finally reaching 961 million *tugriks* during the three-year plan of 1958–60. These figures do not include the assistance provided by foreign countries. If the sums invested by the Soviet Union, Czechoslovakia, and other countries of the Communist bloc are taken into account, the total value of capital investments during the three-year plan alone reaches the formidable figure of 1.3 billion *tugriks*.

The third five-year plan (1961–65) increased the total value of capital investments to 4.46 billion *tugriks*. Not less than 70 per cent of this amount was allocated to the development of industry. Three types of industry received roughly equal portions: industries devoted to the development of energy resources, mostly fuels (31 per cent); food and other light industries (32 per cent); and building-materials industry (29 per cent). The remaining 8 per cent went to miscellaneous industries. The value of capital investment in agriculture during this period was more modest (947.6 million *tugriks*) but represented a substantial increase over the amount allocated to agriculture during the preceding five-year plan—more than twice as much, if the sums used for the development of animal husbandry are included.

The fourth five-year plan was for the period 1966–70. Under it, industrial production was expected to increase 80 per cent over the previous five years. State farms were expected to deliver 30 per cent more grain by 1970 and to produce 2.2 times as much milk. Similar increases were anticipated in other agricultural products.

The history of economic development in Mongolia reveals certain trends that provide clues to the direction industrial production will take in the future. The first major penetration of foreign capital into the country began in 1911, when China declared itself a republic, and Outer Mongolia embarked on a short-lived period of independence. By 1919, there were 363 small Chinese business enterprises in the country, and several large industrial concerns had been established by the Russians, but Mongolian industry was in its infancy then, and although these enterprises employed substantial numbers of Chinese and Russians in addition to Mongols, the total number of workers employed was only about four thousand. A serious attempt to begin producing coal had been made in 1913, when the Nalaikha coal field began operation in the vicinity of Urga, but six years later, in 1919, only forty coal miners were employed in the mines.

The turning point in industrial development did not come about until the early 1920's, when the country was taken over by its Communist leaders with the military assistance of the young Soviet Union. Massive Soviet economic assistance was offered to Mongolia almost at once, not for philanthropic reasons but because the Soviet Union was determined to have a faithful, politically sympathetic satellite on its southern Siberian border. The Soviets confiscated all Russian commercial enterprises in Mongolia and transferred ownership of them to the new Mongolian state. Economic and professional assistance was provided to start new industrial projects, such as the electric power plant in Ulan Bator and two leather-processing factories, but the main effort was concentrated on rebuilding and reconstructing existing industrial enterprises, such as the Nalaikha coal mine, that were either obsolete or whose output was not sufficient to meet the needs of the growing economy.

Substantial, large-scale assistance from the Soviet Union, however, did not begin until 1931, with the construction of large industrial installations, mainly in processing and energy-producing industries. The labor force grew. The number of industrial workers increased from 1,409 in 1930 to 2,064 in 1935. More than half of them were Mongols, whereas in 1927 only 26 per cent of the entire industrial labor force had been natives of Mongolia. The balance of the labor force was, as before, Russian and Chinese. By 1940, when 33,100 workers were employed in Mongolian industry, 87.7 per cent were Mongol, 5.7 per cent were Russian, and 6.6 per cent were Chinese. Twenty years later, the number of industrial workers had increased to 210,000, and in 1963 it was reported that nonagricultural workers and their families comprised 40 per cent of the entire population.

The first major industrial project completed with Soviet aid was a complex of factories for processing leather, for looming and spinning wool, and for manufacturing fur coats. It began operation in 1934. A factory for the production of woolen felt was built in 1936, and one for the manufacture of woolen clothing was started in 1940. Unlike many other countries, Mongolia has geared its industries to animal husbandry and its products. Consequently, emphasis has been on the food industry and on related light industries rather than on heavy industry. Light industry production increased 2.4 times between 1960 and 1965, compared to an increase in heavy industry production of only 1.8 times. Fuel production is the chief heavy industry.

Industrial production increased tenfold between 1940 and 1964. By 1964, industrial output accounted for 41 per cent of the combined output of the country. By a coincidence, 41 per cent of all capital investments made in Mongolia in the same year were in light and heavy industry. The principal share of industrial output (51 per cent) was in light industries, such as the food industry and those involving the processing of raw materials and the products of animal husbandry. Since 1960, the proportion of industrial production of state-owned industries to that of cooperatively owned industries has been fairly constant: about 80 per cent for the former, as compared to 20 per cent for the latter. The growth of both state-owned and cooperative industries for the seven-year period beginning in 1960 is shown in the table.

While it is true that, due to an insufficient trained labor force and a deficient national background, heavy industry lags behind light industry, the processing of mineral resources such as oil and coal and extraction of tungsten, molybdenum, tin, and other minerals have increased. The energy-producing industries are also increasing production.

Value of Industrial Production, 1960–70, Millions of Tugriks

Industry	1960	1962	1963	1964	1965	1967
State-owned	478.1	670.8	716.1	730.9	776.9	941.0
Cooperative	118.4	159.4	174.1	194.9	207.8	267.0
Total production	596.5	830.2	890.2	925.8	984.7	1208.0

SOURCES: *Ekonomika Sotsialisticheskikh Stran v Tsifrakh, 1964* (Economy of Socialist Countries in Statistical Figures, 1964) (Moscow: US.S.R. Academy of Sciences, 1965), p. 158; B. Gungaadash, *Mongoliya Segodnya* (Mongolia Today), (Moscow: 1969), pp. 161–63.

The production of electric power, for instance, doubled in the five years from 1961 to 1966, whereas total industrial production increased only 1.6 times.

It is anticipated that the volume of industrial production will have increased 80 per cent by 1970 at the end of the fourth five-year plan. With the aid of the Soviet Union, Mongolian planners expect to build several installations that will further the development of light industries, particularly the processing of woolen textiles. But heavy industry will receive its share of attention. By the end of the 1960's, the work of expanding operations in the Sharyn Gol coal field will have been concluded with the opening of the new Adunchulum open-pit coal mine. Open-pit mines will begin to produce coal in several other areas of the country. By 1970, the first phase of the construction of a thermal electric power plant in Ulan Bator will have been completed, and the first high-tension power line in Mongolia will have been strung from Ulan Bator, through the new industrial complex at Darkhan, to Sukhe Bator.

9 Industries

The principal industries currently contributing to Mongolia's industrial production are fuel and power, building materials, lumber, chemicals, mining, commercial hunting, fishing, food, and light industries such as leather, soap, and textiles.

Coal

Although the infant oil industry is steadily gaining ground, the main source of fuel for Mongolia's industries and railroads is coal. Only brown coal (lignite), which is dangerous to store because of its combustibility after long periods of storage, has been found so far. The beginning of the coal industry can be traced to 1913, when the Nalaikha coal field, in the vicinity of Urga, began operation. In 1922, the few mines then in existence were nationalized. The Nalaikha field now produces 600,000 metric tons of coal a year. Operations were modernized in 1957 with the technical assistance of Soviet specialists. Opening the new Nalaikha mine at an elevation of 5,000 feet presented great difficulties because it is located in the permafrost zone, where the ground is permanently frozen to a depth of about 150 feet.

The coal mined at Nalaikha is not of first quality, since it produces between 8 and 13 per cent ash and contains between 1 and 2 per cent sulfur. It also has a tendency to break into small particles and is easily pulverized when transported over long distances. However, it is easily combustible. Ten mines are now in operation in the Nalaikha coal basin, where no less than nine coal layers of from 2.5 to 15 feet in thickness have been discovered at various depths.

Approximately ten years ago, the Nalaikha was the only significant coal-producing field in the entire country. Since then, many new fields have been discovered in practically all *aymags* of the republic. The most important of the new fields is the Sharyn Gol, located on the Sharyn Gol River in the northern part of the country. This extensive development was undertaken with the technical assistance of the Soviet Union. Czechoslovakia and Poland helped to build a cement and brick factory, a telephone exchange, and housing for the mine workers. In 1963, the Soviet Union helped to construct a railroad from Darkhan to Sharyn Gol and erected a high-tension power line, thirty-one miles long. The Sharyn Gol coal mine began operation in 1965, and a thermal power plant was completed a year later. The mine has an annual production capacity of 1.1 million tons of coal.

Other coal mines have been opened lately in various parts of the country, the most productive mines being located at Sayn Shanda, Aduun, Chuluu, Yabar, Oldziyt, and Tsagaan Oboo. Coal has also been found in the southern mountains of the Kentei Range, in the Altai Range, and in the northern and southern border regions where the Trans-Mongolian Railroad crosses into the Soviet Union and China. One coal field in the valley of the Muren River, about fifty miles from

Undurkhun, has ricn coal seams up to fifteen feet thick. Even more impressive are the thirty- to eighty-feet-thick seams in the south, about fifteen miles west of the town of Dalan Dzadagad. At least thirteen major coal fields have been discovered. As early as 1961, Mongolia was self-sufficent in coal.

As far as can be judged from the few geological surveys available, Mongolia possesses about 3 billion tons of unmined coal. This is a conservative estimate. Although there has been a steady upswing in production (except in 1964), coal production did not attain the 1964 planned annual goal of over 1 million metric tons until 1967, when 1,250,000 tons were reported.

Oil

The oil industry is comparatively new in Mongolia. It began to make headway only during the second five-year plan (1953–57). The industry is not well developed, and the output of crude oil and other oil products is able to satisfy only about half of Mongolia's oil requirements. Imports from the Soviet Union supply the balance of the country's needs.

The industry received a valuable impetus when the Soviet-owned Mongolneft Oil Survey and Exploitation Company transferred its equipment free of charge to Mongolia. One of the first operating oil fields, south of the town of Sayn Shanda in the eastern Gobi region, started producing oil in 1951. Not far away, at Dzunbayn in East Gobi *aymag,* an oil refinery was built with Soviet technical and financial assistance to produce gasoline and other crude oil products obtained from the field at Sayn Shanda. Dzunbayn, in the heart of the Gobi Desert, promises to be the center of the Mongolian oil extraction industry. The city, which has sprung up around the refinery, is still growing.

The total annual production of oil fluctuates from 18,000 to 20,000 tons, although these figures may be conservative in view of the claims that are sometimes made that the Sayn Shanda field produces 30,000 tons annually. Known deposits of oil shale, a potential source of oil products, have been discovered, mainly in two regions—the Central Gobi and South Gobi *aymags*.

Electric Power

The generation of electric power in Mongolia is closely tied to the coal industry, since the power plants use coal as fuel. The power industry spurted ahead in the middle 1960's with the creation of a new industrial complex in Darkhan, formerly little more than a small railroad station on the Trans-Mongolian Railroad, about 150 miles north of Ulan Bator. The development of this area has been assisted by practically all members of COMECON (the Council for Mutual Assistance, uniting the separate national economies of the Soviet bloc countries), with the Soviet Union in the lead. A large thermal power plant is one of the major industrial projects under way at Darkhan. It will have a planned generating capacity of 100,000 kilowatts.

In 1924, the thermal power plant in Ulan Bator was the only electric power plant in the entire country. It generated 60 kilowatts, most of which was for household use. When the Ulan Bator Mechanical Works was built in 1928, a new plant was constructed with a capacity of 110 kilowatts. This was increased to 500 kilowatts in 1931. Three years later, when a new industrial complex was built in the capital, a larger electric power plant was constructed, with a capacity of 2,500 kilowatts, a considerable achievement for Mongolia in those days. The generating capacity of this plant was more than doubled in 1939. By 1963, the total generating capacity of all the electric power plants in Ulan Bator had reached 35,000 kilowatts. In 1965, the figure stood at 60,000. Next in rank were the thermal electric power plants at Sukhe Bator (6,000 kilowatts) and the plant at Choibalsan (3,000 kilowatts).

The plant at Darkhan, when completed, will supply power not only for forty local industries and the coal mining operations at the nearby Sharyn Gol mines, but will also supply power over high-tension lines to various cities, towns, and settlements some distance away. Sukhe Bator will be the first large city to so benefit. When the power plant and other constructions under way at Darkhan are completed, this former settlement will be the second largest industrial city in Mongolia. By the end of the 1960's, Mongolia should have a total electrical generating capacity of about 200,000 kilowatts, with an output of 440 million kilowatt-hours.

Building Materials

The building-materials industry is the fastest-growing branch of industry in Mongolia because of the rapid growth of new cities and the expansion of old cities and towns. Housing is needed to take care of the new urban populations. The overall production of building materials increased an estimated ten times between 1947 and 1960. The production of building materials represents about 11 per cent of the country's total industrial production, and it is estimated that 6 per cent of the country's labor force is engaged in the building-materials industry. The most important materials are brick, limestone, and felt. The last is used in large quantities to cover the frames of *yurts,* round tents that still dot the Mongolian landscape. However, the type of building materials produced in Mongolia is constantly increasing. There is now substantial production of glass, silicate, tile, cement, and concrete. Poland and Czechoslavakia are assisting in the construction of cement and silicate plants in the industrial complex at Darkhan. A plant specializing in the production of prefabricated concrete panels has already been built at Darkhan. A new factory for the construction of prefabricated housing panels has been constructed in Ulan Bator; it is capable of manufacturing panels to provide 70,000 square meters of housing space a year.

Lumber

The timber resources of Mongolia are reported to represent a formidable 1.25 billion cubic meters, of which 1 billion cubic meters are located in the northern, mountainous region. Khubsugul and Kentei are the most suitable areas for the future development of the lumber industry. It would be possible to cut 4.5 million cubic meters there, without harming the country's timber resources. Much lumber is shipped down the Orkhon, Selenga, and Kerulen rivers. To take full advantage of Mongolia's timber resources would require a good transportation network, which the country lacks, but with the completion of the Trans-Mongolian Railroad in 1950, a beginning was made. The timber industry accounts for 13 per cent of Mongolia's total industrial production. The principal users of lumber are the wood-processing plants. These include the furniture factory at Ulan Bator, a factory for making prefabricated houses at Sukhe Bator (it provides units for more than 20,000 square meters of living space a year), and two prefabrication factories built with Soviet aid in 1960 in the Dzabkhan and the Uber Khangai *aymags,* each with a capacity of 1,500 standard houses a year. Lumber waste from these factories is used in the manufacture of paper and matches. The country's first paper factory, constructed recently, has a total annual output of 3,500 tons of newsprint, wrapping paper, and cardboard.

Chemicals

Although Mongolia possesses a great variety of suitable raw materials, the country's chemical industry is in its infancy. One of the largest enterprises in this field is the oil refinery in Dzun Bayn. A plant located at Choreyn produces 950,000 gallons of industrial alcohol a year. The pharmaceutical plant in Ulan Bator employs 500 full-time workers. Twenty-five miles from the capital is a factory, built with the aid of Hungary, that manufactures biochemicals, mainly to supply the needs of veterinarians.

Mining

Except for the mining of coal, mining in Mongolia is concerned mainly with the extraction of minerals and mineral ore for export, which provides "foreign currency" for the country. A large metallurgical center for the extraction of iron ore is planned for the industrial complex at Darkhan, but the emphasis so far has been on nonferrous metals, principally tungsten, molybdenum, and manganese, which are mined chiefly in the Kentei and Sukhe Bator *aymags*. A new tungsten mine, expected to be one of the most important in the country, was opened recently in the Zorgal Khairkhan Mountains near the Gobi Desert. Tungsten is also found in the Central *aymag,* as is tin. Manganese is found in the South Gobi, East Gobi, and Central *aymags*. There are considerable deposits of copper near Khubsugul Lake, in the Khangai Mountains, and in the east Gobi and Bayan Khongor *aymags*. Lead and silver are mined in the Kentei Mountains, in Khangai, and in the Mongolian Altai and Gobi Altai ranges. Some lead and silver deposits are also found near Khubsugul Lake.

Commercial Hunting

Hunting is one of the oldest occupations of the Mongols. The country is rich in wild birds and animals, particularly fur-bearing animals such as sable, ermine, otter, squirrel, and lynx, which inhabit the northern and western mountain regions. The steppes and mixed forest-steppe zones abound in tarbagan, a variety of woodchuck, whose fur is the country's leading fur export. About 2.1 million tarbagan pelts are processed annually. Squirrel, fox, Tatar fox, and wolf furs are also processed in great numbers.

Fishing

Fishing is still in a primitive stage in Mongolia, although recently several modern concerns have been organized for the purpose of putting fishing on a commercial basis in the lakes and rivers of the country. The fish population has hardly been touched, which points to a long and bright future for the industry. An annual catch of 30,000 metric tons is possible with modern methods of fishing—a far cry from the present annual catch, which is between 800 and 1,000 tons.

The most promising fishery areas are Khubsugul Lake, which could provide up to 500 tons of fish a year, and the water basins of the Shihshid Gol, where several lakes in the area are capable of yielding a total annual catch of 350 tons. The most promising region for commercial fishing, however, is in the east, Buir Nur, where up to 1,200 tons of fish a year is a reasonable prospect.

Cooperative Industries

About 18 per cent of the total industrial production of Mongolia comes from small cooperatives of artisans who use local raw materials. The products of cooperative industries are mostly consumer goods, such as footwear, clothing, *yurts,* and carpets. Ceramics and embroidery are also produced by cooperative societies.

The Food Industry

Mongolia's food industry employs about 15 per cent of the labor force of the country but is responsible for more than 25 per cent of the total industrial production. It concentrates on the processing of milk products (about 41 per cent of the total food industry production) and meat products (about 14 per cent of the total).

Dairy products are produced by a multitude of small farms spread all over the country, but concentrated in the east. Most of them are primitive and their products, butter in particular, must be refined and upgraded in Ulan Bator. Modern dairies were first constructed in 1940, and the number of modern dairies is now close to three hundred. The largest of these, in Ulan Bator, is able to process 35 tons of milk and 6 tons of cream a day.

One of the largest, most modern food industry enterprises is the meat-packing plant in Ulan Bator, constructed in 1946 with the assistance of the Soviet Union. It has a daily capacity of 800 head of small animals and 300 head of large cattle. The total annual production of the meat-packing industry is over 17,000 tons a year. The comparatively new flour milling industry has grown as the amount of tillable acreage has increased. The recently constructed flour mill in Ulan Bator can process over 31,000 tons of flour a year. Its grain elevator has a capacity of 16,000 tons. Other flour mills, with an average capacity of 3,000 tons of flour per year, are scattered throughout the country, but mainly in the grain-growing regions of Ubsunur, Eastern, and Bulgan *aymags*. The combined annual production of flour in Mongolia is about 70,000 tons. A factory-size bakery in Ulan Bator produces 5,000 tons of bakery products a year.

Light Industries

Light industries (other than the food industry) account for more than 25 per cent of the total industrial production of Mongolia. The Ulan Bator industrial combine, which produces more than 1.3 million pieces of leather annually, is the most important Mongolian enterprise in this category. It has recently been reconstructed with the aid of specialists from Czechoslovakia. An artificial leather plant, also reconstructed recently and supplied with Soviet, Czechoslovak, and East German machinery, is now capable of manufacturing 370,000 pairs of shoes a year and between 350 and 400 tons of shoe soles.

Other light industries in Ulan Bator include a print shop, built with aid of East Germany, and a soap factory with a daily capacity of 4.8 tons of household soap and 12,000 cakes of toilet soap. The match factory in Sukhe Bator produces 30 million boxes of matches a year. Darkhan has a textile factory (producing 70 million feet of textiles a year), a kid-leather factory (4 million feet a year), and a carpet factory (with projected production figures of about 600,000 feet a year).

10 Agriculture

In spite of recent industrial progress, it will be many years before industry replaces agriculture, primarily animal husbandry, as the basis of Mongolia's economy. The traditionally nomadic population has depended on livestock-raising for many centuries. Out of a total land area of 385.5 million acres, 358 million acres are usable as grazing lands. Only 4.5 million acres are suitable for cultivation, with 3.7 million additional acres being good for the production of hay. Of the acreage suitable for cultivation, nearly 3.5 million acres remain virgin land. In 1965, the total cultivated area was a bit over 1 million acres—a small part of Mongolia's total area but a significant increase over the 172,900 acres under cultivation at the time Mongolia acquired its independence.

Mongolia as a whole suffers from a lack of water. About half of the land area is not suitable for either animal husbandry or cultivation. Of the 358 million acres of potential grazing lands, only 62 per cent has enough water to sustain livestock. There is wide variation in the percentage of usable grazing lands from one region to another. Ara Khangai *aymag,* for instance, which has rivers, lakes, and underground water reserves, is able to use 84 per cent of its grazing land, whereas Choibalsan *aymag* has only enough water to sustain livestock on 34 per cent of its potential grazing lands.

Irrigation would make cultivation possible in many parts of Mongolia, particularly in the areas between the Orkhon and the Selenga rivers, as well as along the valleys of streams south of the Great Lakes Depression, in the valleys of the Onon, Kerulen, and Khalkin Gol rivers in the far east, in the river valleys of the Kentei zone, and even in the semi-desert Gobi area. However, the total irrigated area is small —about 60,000 acres—two-thirds of which are lands belonging to the state farms. The remaining lands under irrigation are in the agricultural cooperatives or are part of experimental agricultural stations administered by the Mongolian Academy of Sciences.

Collectivization

The transition from an almost feudal economy to socialization was not an easy one. Most Mongols in the early 1920's were nomadic horsemen or cattlemen, who migrated from grazing land to grazing land. The nomads had to be brought under state control, and, according to the government, animal husbandry and farming had to be collectivized before progress could be made. The change was to be made on the basis of experiments with state farms and cooperatives in the Soviet Union, but placing Mongol nomads in collective farms was far more difficult than collectivizing peasants in Russia.

Before collectivization, half of Mongolia's livestock belonged to 7.8 per cent of the total population, a group composed of the nobility and the priestly class. The other half of the livestock was distributed among the rest of the population. Collectivization was resisted by the propertied classes and the peasants and nomads. It could not proceed without official "persuasion," and the process led to an appalling loss of both human and animal life. During the Lama Rebellion of 1932, many nomads slaughtered hundreds of thousands of their livestock and made their way into China. It has been estimated that one-third of the livestock in Mongolia was killed in this effort to resist collectivization.

However, the process was brought to its inevitable conclusion, and in 1959 the rulers of Mongolia proudly proclaimed the completion of collectivization. It was announced that the entire agricultural population had been fully "socialized" into either state-owned farms or agricultural cooperatives.

The importance of state farms in the national economy is apparent from the fact that they produce about 80 per cent of all grains obtained by the state and have become the grain "factories" of Mongolia, which fifty years ago had practically no grain crops or granaries. Animal husbandry is not neglected on the farms. High-grade sheep and pedigree cattle and horses are bred on them, and 60 per cent of Mongolia's fine wool comes from them. The state and the ruling party consider state farms the country's primary agencies for the modernization of farming and animal husbandry.

In 1940, there were three state farms. By 1952, the number had increased to twelve. At the present time there are thirty-one, with an average of 42,500 acres of cultivatable land each and 332,000 acres of grazing and grassland. They are patterned after Soviet state farms, which use modern mechanized equipment. Each Mongolian state farm therefore has seventy or more tractors and about fifty combines for harvesting grain. There are three types of state farms: (1) those devoted to grain farming exclusively; (2) those that raise grain and also engage in animal husbandry, mainly the breeding of sheep and pigs; and (3) those that specialize in vegetable growing and milk production.

Unlike the agricultural cooperatives, which are rather evenly distributed throughout the country, state farms are located in regions of virgin land, which is converted to agricultural use. Half are in the northern part of the country, principally the Central and Bulgan *aymags;* about 20 per cent are in the eastern region, chiefly in the Eastern and Kentei *aymags.* State farms are usually located in areas with adequate precipitation or available ground water. Although they occupy only about 2 per cent of the land area of Mongolia, they encompass about 80 per cent of the cultivatable land—but only 1.5 per cent of the available grazing land, which is mostly under the control of the agricultural cooperatives.

The agricultural cooperatives account for 55 per cent of Mongolia's total agricultural production. They supply 86 per cent of all meat purchased by the state and 72 per cent of the milk. However, the contribution in wool (17 per cent) and grain (14 per cent) is much less than that of the state farms.

By 1955, collectivization was in full swing. More than 99 per cent of all households belonged to cooperatives. The cooperatives were small in size at first, but by 1959 they had been consolidated into 389 larger units, holding almost three-fourths of the country's livestock. The process of consolidation continued, until by 1963 there were approximately three hundred cooperatives, each with an average of 60,000 head of livestock and 1 million acres of land. In the process of collectivization, all cattle, horses, sheep, and other domestic animals became communal property, but each household, which takes care of approximately 100 head of livestock for the cooperative, is allowed to have 24 head for its own use and more if it is located in the desert-like Gobi region. One of the drawbacks to animal husbandry in Mongolia had been its dependence on year-round grazing. Many animals, unable to obtain fodder from under the snow in severe winters, died. The agricultural cooperatives have tried to reduce this loss by harvesting about 1 million metric tons of hay each year and storing it for use during the winter months. This has encouraged the switch from the migratory type of livestock raising to the mixed grazing-corral type. The animals still spend twelve months a year in the open, but they are protected in winter by lean-tos or walls that shelter them from the biting north winds.

Mechanization has brought additional change to Mongolia's rural economy. There are now forty-one stations in Mongolia that provide enough tractors and combines to carry out 95 per cent of all field work for the cooperatives, from plowing to harvesting. They are patterned on the former machine-tractor stations in the Soviet Union (which were eventually transformed into machine-repair stations). Mechanization of agriculture is dependent on the goodwill and assistance of Mongolia's northern neighbor. The Soviet Union has supplied the country with agricultural specialists and has brought in tractors and other agricultural machinery to equip the stations. In 1952, there were 215 tractors and 37 grain combines in Mongolia. During the next six years, these numbers increased to 1,527 and 390, and six years later, in 1964, there were 7,800 tractors and 1,889 combines.

Animal Husbandry

Animal husbandry accounts for approximately 80 per cent of the total agricultural production of Mongolia—a considerable contribution to the nation's economy, since agricultural products constitute about half of the country's total production.

By 1958, the shortage of livestock that had resulted from forced collectivization had been overcome. In 1965, there were approximately twenty-seven head of livestock per person, compared to twenty per person in 1924. This was the largest number of livestock per capita of any country in the world.

Sheep and goats comprise most of the livestock in Mongolia, but the Mongols also raise substantial numbers of cattle, horses, and camels. In the high-altitude Khubsugul area of northwestern Mongolia, yaks are raised, and in this same region some attention is being given to the raising and breeding of reindeer.

The importance of sheep in the economy of Mongolia cannot be overestimated. This animal comprises more than half of the country's livestock and provides wool, meat, milk, and skins. Sheep's wool is the country's major item of export. Mongolian sheep are hardy and well acclimatized to the severe winters and dry summers. In addition to not being as demanding as most other domestic animals in their food requirements, they are able to travel long distances between pastures. They are also able to consume the low-grade grasses found in desert, semidesert, and high mountain regions. The sheep-raising industry is therefore evenly distributed throughout the country, although there is a slight concentration in the western areas, where sheep and goats represent 80 per cent of all livestock, and in the southern Gobi region, where they constitute 75 per cent of all domestic animals.

Goats, which constitute about 25 per cent of the country's livestock, are even less demanding than sheep in their grazing requirements and are capable of grazing on high mountain slopes, where the grass is of poor quality. Goats are found mainly in the south and west, in the desert and semidesert zones and in practically all the mountainous regions. They are more numerous than sheep in the South Gobi *aymag*. Regions that concentrate on the raising of goats in Mongolia raise practically no cattle. The principal products derived from goats are milk and wool and, to some extent, meat.

Although cattle are not as numerous in Mongolia as sheep and goats are, as a source of meat and milk products (mainly butter) they are second only to sheep in importance in the country's agricultural economy. Mongolian cattle are usually small and weigh between 700 and 900 pounds. The annual milk production per cow is between 635 and 845 gallons. Cattle are found in every part of the country, but the main concentrations are in the north-central and eastern regions, where the pastures are comparatively rich and there is abundant water. Yaks usually graze at elevations between 6,500 and 10,000 feet above sea level on land inaccessible to cows.

They produce slightly less milk per capita than cows do, and their milk has a higher fat content. Horses have always been important in the nomadic society of Mongolia. It has been estimated that, from the days of Genghis Khan until about twenty years ago, at least one hundred thousand horses were always in use in Mongolia for transportation and hauling. By 1949, however, the automobile and other types of mechanized transport had practically replaced the horse as a means of transportation. The 2.5 million horses in the country today represent about 10 per cent of the country's livestock. They are used not only for riding but also for meat and mare's milk. Each mare produces from 190 to 210 gallons of milk a year, which is valued not only as a milk product but also for its medicinal qualities. Mare's milk is used in the preparation of *kumys*, a fermented milk product, of which more than 10 million gallons are produced each year. Horses are distributed more or less evenly throughout the country, with the exception of the mountainous areas in the west and the desert regions in the south.

The nine hundred thousand camels in Mongolia represent nearly 4 per cent of the livestock and are of exceptional importance in the desert and semidesert areas. They consume the sparse desert vegetation and drink brackish or salt water and so manage to survive in places where no other domestic animals can exist. Mongolian camels can get along without water for up to twelve days if necessary. The cultivation of the semidesert regions would have been impossible without them.

Mongolian camels are of the Bactrian, two-hump, type rather the one-hump type common in Arab lands. They can carry between 400 and 525 pounds and, when hitched to a two-wheel cart, can pull between 650 and 1,300 pounds of cargo. As a beast of burden, the Mongolian camel's speed is as much as twenty-five miles a day.

The camel is a source of milk and meat, particularly in the Gobi regions. A camel ordinarily provides about eleven pounds of wool a year. About 18 per cent of the total wool production in Mongolia is camel wool. Camels are distributed throughout the desert and semidesert areas. In the East Gobi, South Gobi, Central Gobi, and Uber Khangai *aymags*, they account for 13 per cent of the livestock. More than half of the camels in Mongolia are in these four *aymags*.

Farming

Isolated attempts to make nomads farmers were made as early as 1930, but the Mongols preferred to remain herdsmen. To compel wandering tribesmen into work they had traditionally scorned was difficult. In 1924, Mongolia's Communist rulers were faced with the fact that only 25,000 acres of land had been plowed. By 1937, there was an increase to 42,950 acres, but this increase was due not to the Mongols but to the effort of Chinese peasants, who had plowed more than 90 per cent of all farmed land in the nation. In 1940, less than 5 per cent of all Mongol households considered farming their primary occupation. Even today, only a small proportion of households in the agricultural cooperatives are engaged in farming, and most of the country's grain-growing must be entrusted to the state farms.

Grain is grown on 90 per cent of all the cultivated land in Mongolia. Four-fifths of this crop is wheat. Mongolia has been self-sufficient in the production of flour since 1960. In that year, Mongolia's own grain requirements had been met to such an extent that the nation was able to export 25 per cent of the harvest. Oats are the second largest grain crop. Other grains grown are barley and, since 1955, corn. By 1957, 7,400 acres were planted in corn, and in 1960, 49,400 acres were devoted to this crop. The increase in grain production between 1957 and 1964 was enormous. The 1957 harvest yielded 116.6 pounds of grain for each inhabitant of Mongolia. By 1964, the per capita amount had increased to 770 pounds. This progress was made possible by the massive assistance rendered by the Soviet Union, which supplied Mongolia with agricultural specialists as well as machinery.

11 Transportation and Communications

The main routes in Mongolia were established centuries ago to provide the shortest, most convenient connection between the capital (formerly Urga) and Russia, China, and the outlying regions of Mongolia. One of the most traveled of these was the Kalgan-Urga-Kyakhta route, which cut across the country from China to the Russian border and on to Verkhneudinsk (now Ulan Ude) in eastern Siberia, a total of 840 miles. A longer route covered the 1,050 miles between Urga and Ulyassutai. Manchouli Station, the western terminal of the former Chinese Eastern Railway in Manchuria, was connected to Urga by a 620-mile caravan route. Another important route, 500 miles long, connected Kalgan to Guchen by way of Ulyassutai. Other routes connected the capital with Huh Hoto in Inner Mongolia. All of these ancient caravan routes played a vital role in connecting Mongolia with the outside world in the days before the Chinese Eastern Railway in Manchuria and the Trans-Siberian Railway in Siberia became the main connecting link between Mongolia and Europe.

More than 70 per cent of the freight formerly carried on the back of pack animals or in camel-drawn carts is now carried by railroads, but this does not mean that Mongolia is crisscrossed by a dense network of rails. On the contrary, nearly all of this freight travels over one route, running north to south by way of Ulan Bator. A few shorter railroads to the east of the main line account for the rest of the rail traffic. The total length of all the railroads in Mongolia is about 1,000 miles.

The first steps in modernizing the transportation system of Mongolia were taken at the end of the 1920's, when roads with hard surfaces were first built. The construction of railroads did not begin until much later. The first railroad was a narrow-gauge line, about 27 miles long, connecting Ulan Bator with the Nalaikha coal mine. Construction was completed in 1938. In 1939, a broad-gauge railroad from Solovievsk to Choibalsan, a distance of 147 miles, was constructed, connecting the industrial center of eastern Mongolia with Borzya Station of the Trans-Siberian Railway. Construction of this line proved to be very timely. In 1939, it was used to transport the Soviet and Mongolian troops that repulsed the massive incursion of the Japanese troops from Manchuria in the battle of the Khalkin Gol River. In 1945, this line was continued, as a narrow-gauge railroad from Choibalsan to Ulan Dzuleg, where it divided into two branches, to Tamsag Bulag and to Dzun Bulag.

World War II, although not directly involving Mongolia, nevertheless halted further construction of railroads. The construction of railroads in Mongolia was financed by the Soviet Union, which, at death grips with Hitler's Germany, could not spare a single rail to Mongolia, so urgent was the need for men and materials to assist in the titanic struggle for its own survival. Not until 1947, two years after the termination of World War II, was Mongolia, with the aid of the Soviet Union, able to start construction of the Ulan Bator Railway from Naushki on the Soviet border to Ulan Bator. The 258-mile line became fully operative in 1950. It proved to be a great boon to the economic life of the country, not only because it connected the capital and the Soviet Union but because it crossed the area of the major economic activity of Mongolia. It released 16,000 trucks and 40,000 animal-drawn carts for use on other routes to remote regions of the country.

The next important project in railroad construction was inaugurated in 1952, when an agreement was signed between the Soviet Union and Mongolia to provide for the construction of the railroad from Ulan Bator to Dzamun Uude on the Mongolian-Chinese border, a distance of 440 miles. This line, completed in 1955, provided a direct link between the Soviet Union and China, by way of Mongolia, and reduced the traveling distance between Moscow and Peking by 707 miles. The total length of the Ulan Bator Railway through Mongolia from Naushki on the Soviet border to Dzamun Uude on the Chinese border is about 700 miles.

The north-to-south Ulan Bator Railway, more often referred to as the Trans-Mongolian Railroad, is the backbone of the country's transportation system. It is supplemented by a long highway that stretches across the country from east to west. These two arteries carry most of the country's freight —the products of animal husbandry, building materials, machine equipment, oil products, grain, coal, and ores.

The importance of the railroads in Mongolia's economy is great. One freight train, making the run from Ulan Bator to the Russian border in less than one day, can carry as much cargo as was formerly carried by eight thousand camels covering the same distance in fifteen days. The comparison is even more startling if all 700 miles of the Trans-Mongolian Railroad, from the Russian border to the Chinese border, are considered. A diesel-driven freight train can make the trip in one and a half days. It would take ten thousand camels ninety days to carry the same amount of freight the same distance.

Aside from its principal function as freight carrier, the railroad system of Mongolia serves as a rapid transportation link between such political, economic, and cultural centers as Ulan Bator, Sukhe Bator, and Sayn Shanda. It also provides work for thousands of former nomads and herdsmen, who have become railroad technicians and workers. The railroad technical school in Ulan Bator, founded in 1952, trains technicians. Engineers and members of more skilled professions required for the operation of the railroad are trained in the institutions of higher learning in the Soviet Union and other countries of the Communist bloc.

The total length of all railroads in Mongolia is only about 1,000 miles, but there are approximately 5,000 miles of hard-surface and improved highways and about 50,000 miles of unimproved roads suitable for use by trucks and passenger automobiles. The first asphalt highway was built in 1940 between Ulan Bator and Sukhe Bator, a distance of 207 miles, and it is still one of the major highways of Mongolia. Other major highways connect the capital to Kobdo, Choibalsan, Sayn Shanda, and Dalan Dzadagad. Communist China has provided much assistance in highway construction on the basis of an agreement signed with Mongolia in 1956.

China has built dozens of pedestrian and vehicular bridges in addition to highways.

The beginnings of automobile transport in Mongolia go back to 1930, when the Soviet-Mongolian Transport Company was formed to carry freight into the country in trucks and other automotive vehicles. In 1936, the Soviet government transferred all shares in the company and all property and equipment to the Mongolian government as a gift. The role of automobile transport in the economy has greatly increased since World War II. At the present, more than three-fourths of all local cargoes are carried by auto transport.

The seventy-five miles of waterways in Mongolia are a minor part of the country's transportation system. The Selenga River, which flows into the Soviet Union, and Khubsugul Lake are the principal water routes. The shipment of freight by water lags far behind shipments by rail and highway but has been increasing. Between 1958 and 1960 it increased by 30 per cent. Cargoes transported by water are chiefly bulky goods such as grain and building materials.

Trade between the Soviet Union and Mongolia is conducted almost entirely by water. The first steamer to appear on Khubsugul Lake was Russian. That was in 1913. By 1926, shipping had begun on the Selenga and Orkhon rivers for a distance of about 120 miles. In 1953, the Soviet Union transferred all its holdings in the shipping company to the Mongolian government.

Air transportation in Mongolia was initiated in 1926 with the signing of an agreement with the Soviet Union that provided for the establishment of an air line between Ulan Bator and Verkhneudinsk in eastern Siberia. Regular air service with Moscow was inaugurated in 1945, using Soviet planes. All facilities for air transport in Mongolia have been constructed by the Soviets. However, as in the case of rail and water shipping, all facilities for air transport, such as airfields, hangars, runways, and four planes, were eventually given to Mongolia. Later, the Soviet Union furnished technical and financial assistance for the construction of a jetport at Ulan Bator. Regular flights are now made to Moscow, Peking, Irkutsk in Siberia, and Hanoi in North Vietnam. Originally, all pilots on Mongolian air lines were Russian. Since 1959, Mongolian pilots have been employed on all local and international flights. In that year, 700 tons of mail and 30,000 passengers were carried. Five years later, the number of passengers had increased to 100,000 and the weight of air freight had reached 2 million tons. The annual rate of increase in the number of passengers is now about 12 per cent. Air lines serve every *aymag* of the country. On these and on international flights, Soviet-built planes are generally used.

The communication system of Mongolia has greatly improved in recent years. Postal service was initiated in Mongolia in 1863, when a few Russian merchants in Urga organized more or less regular postal deliveries between Kyakhta on the Russian border and Kalgan in northern China. Although this service was financed by private commercial firms, the Russian government, which had designs on Mongolia, added three additional routes. In 1913, the Russian postal service was reorganized and replaced by the Chinese with a system running from north to south and east to west. Letters were delivered twice a month and parcels once a month.

In the early 1920's, the automobile replaced animals as

the means of mail delivery for areas not serviced by the railroads. Boats and planes are also used. On the whole, the
postal service in Mongolia has progressed from one of the
country's most backward services to one of its most modern.

The progress of the telegraph service roughly parallels
that of the mails. The first overland telegraph cable was laid
by a Danish company at the end of the nineteenth century
between Kyakhta and Peking. This inspired the Russians
to obtain the rights to a 250-mile line between Kosh Agach
and Kobdo in western Mongolia. The next telegraph line
was installed by the Russians in 1914 and ran 372 miles,
from Mondy to Ulyassutai. It was followed by a new cable
between Kyakhta and Kalgan, by way of Urga, and practically paralleled the line of the Danish company. When the
Soviet government came to power, it transferred all 1,500
miles of telegraph lines and associated buildings and equipment to the Mongols.

Recently, several additional underground cables and overhead lines have been installed. A direct telegraph line now
connects Ulan Bator with Kobdo. An international cable
has been laid across Mongolia, and a line has been strung
along the Trans-Mongolian Railroad. At the present, there
are about 1,200 miles of cable and more than 20,000 miles of
overhead telegraph lines, giving the capital direct communication with Moscow, Peking, Prague, and other capitals of
the world.

Telephone service in Mongolia has progressed as much as
mail and telegraph services. The small telephone exchange
in Urga and with sixty clients, built by Russians in 1915, has
become the modern telephone exchange in Ulan Bator,
providing both domestic and international service. It con-

nects the capital of the country with all *aymag* centers, all agricultural cooperatives, and all state farms. Mongolia is still far behind the rest of the world in terms of the number of telephone exchanges and individual telephones, but more are being installed every year. The number of telephone exchanges increased 85 per cent between 1960 and 1966. The number of automatic telephone exchanges serving the cities, state farms, and agricultural cooperatives is supposed to be greatly increased.

In 1934, the first broadcasts were made from a new Mongolian radio broadcasting station in Ulan Bator, built with the aid of the Soviet Union. This station was rather small in the beginning, but its power was increased to 100 kilowatts in 1952. The introduction of radio led to a new business, the sale of receiving sets manufactured, for the most part, in the Soviet Union. Radio is now an integral part of everyday life in Mongolia. There are seventeen radio broadcasting stations and more than 21,000 radio receivers in the country.

12 The People

Only recently did Mongolia's population reach 1 million. By January, 1970, there were 1,227,800 people in the country. About 90 per cent are Mongols, but it is not incorrect to call Mongolia a multinational state. Located in the heart of Asia at the crossroads of Central Asia's caravan trails, Mongolia has for centuries been the scene of the meeting and mingling of migrating people and as a result has a mixture of races and nationalities.

At least twelve groups can be distinguished by differences in language. One major linguistic group, the Altaic, is divided into three important subgroups: Mongolic, Turkic, and Tungus-Manchurian. About 90 per cent of the population is in the Mongolic language group, which is divided into several national groups, the largest of which is the Khalkha Mongols (75.6 per cent of the entire population). The Khalkhas are concentrated in the Khangai region, but they also occupy a considerable portion of the country from the eastern boundaries to the Mongolian Altai Range. They have preserved their customs, language, and traditions, practically unchanged, since ancient times. The western part of the country is occupied by another member of the Mongolic linguistic group, the Oirats, who comprise slightly more than 7 per cent of the entire population. Their language, quite different from that of the Khalkha Mongols, is a mixture of Mongolian with words borrowed from the Turkic languages. The Turkic linguistic group is represented by the Kazakhs and Tuvinians. The Kazakhs (4.3 per cent of the total population) live in the extreme western section of the country and are administratively grouped into a single *aymag*—the Bayan Ulegey Kazakh national *aymag*. The Tuvinians (1.9 per cent of the population) live mainly in the Kobdo Valley.

The third and smallest of the Altaic linguistic subgroups, the Tungus-Manchurian, is found principally in the northeastern part of the country.

Chinese and Russian are spoken by some people in Mongolia. The Chinese began to move into the country at the end of the seventeenth century, establishing agricultural settlements in what are now the Selenga and Central *aymags*. The Russians, who comprise about 1 per cent of the total population, arrived more recently than the Chinese. They began to drift into Mongolia at the end of the eighteenth century. Many were refugees from Siberia or escapees from Siberian penal colonies. They settled along the valleys of the Selenga and Orkhon rivers.

For centuries, most Mongols have lived as nomadic herdsmen, constantly on the move in search of grazing land with adequate water supplies for their herds. For these people, each season has its particular chore. When spring arrives, the *arats* (herdsmen) and their livestock are usually on the southern slopes of the mountain ranges, where they are protected from the biting north winds. When the warm summer weather arrives, they move their herds in the direction of the river valleys or into the mountains, where the grass is green and juicy. May or June is sheep-shearing time, the cows have calved and milking begins. By the end of June, the milking of mares has begun and with it the preparation of fermented mare's milk. In September, the second sheep-shearing begins. With fall, which comes rather early in Mongolia, the *arats* move their herds to new locations, where there is less protection against the winds. The wind tends to sweep away the swarms of autumn insects that attack the livestock. In winter, the *arats* move into the sheltered valleys where the animals are protected from winter winds. Crude structures of wood and rock walls with partial roofs are the only shelters built for the animals at this time of year. With the return of spring comes the yearly move to the warm southern slopes of the mountains, and the cycle begins again.

The system of feeding the animals has undergone some changes since collectivization. However, in most cases, livestock continues to forage for itself, and in this constant search for fodder, the majority of the *arats* still live the nomadic life of their ancestors—except that now they are members of cooperatives and the ownership of the animals is mostly communal.

The face of Mongolia has been changing. The growth of the urban population is an important reason for the change. In preindependence days, only 2 per cent of the total population of Mongolia could be classed as urban, and these urban dwellers were mainly foreigners, members of various trading companies, officials of missions, foreign nationals at consulates, and the like. Ever since independence, however, the proportion of urban to rural population has been steadily on the rise. In 1927, only 13 per cent of the population lived in cities. Thirty years later, the urban population was 27.5 per cent of the total, and figures for 1967 indicate that 40.5 per cent of all Mongolians now live in cities.

About two-thirds of the country's urban population is concentrated in Ulan Bator, the capital, which holds almost one-fourth of the country's entire population, about 270,000 people. The remaining urban population is spread among twenty-three settlements with populations of more than 3,000, principally in the larger *aymag* centers and the industrial cities that have come into existence during the last few decades: Sukhe Bator; Choibalsan; and Kobdo; as well as Nalaikha, the center of the Nalaikha coal-mining industry; Dzunbayn, the center of the oil industry; Sayn Shanda in the Gobi Desert; and Darkhan, the new industrial complex in the north, which already has a population of more than 40,000.

Although the Mongols are traditionally nomadic, they have a long history of city construction. The first Mongolian cities of note were constructed in the seventh century A.D., during the days of the Uigur state. In 1220, the city of Karakorum was built on the banks of the Orkhon River and served as the glittering capital of the empire of Genghis Khan and his successors until it was leveled in the following century when the Chinese armies of the Ming Dynasty overran Mongolia. Many of the present cities, such as Ulan Bator and Choibalsan (formerly Bain Tyumen), were originally monasteries, which served for centuries as cultural centers. Cities in the border regions, such as Ulyassutai and Kobdo, usually grew up around fortresses or former forts.

Housing reflects the mingling of the traditional and the modern in Mongolia. The nomadic life in Mongolia requires a special type of shelter, which is a tent that can be easily folded up and packed on the back of a camel or other pack-animal. Agricultural cooperatives have introduced new modes of living, but the *yurt* (felt tent) is still the dominant form of housing in rural Mongolia. It can be set up in half an hour. The frame consists of from four to six flexible panels of wooden slats, placed on the ground in a circle and joined at the top by wooden poles, which provide a conical roof with an opening at the peak through which smoke from the hearth inside the tent escapes. The frame is covered with layers of felt, over which a strong white material is placed and attached with ropes.

A typical Mongolian *yurt* has an open fireplace in the center of the floor. Only one type of fuel was available in early times for use by nomads in the steppes—dried cattle dung. Directly opposite the entrance to the *yurt* was an altar, generally nothing more elaborate than a high wooden box, on which revered images and statues were placed.

Many older nomads still prefer the crowded warmth of a *yurt* on a cold winter's night to a modern house. At sundown, the tent will suddenly be filled to capacity, not only by the members of the family and their guests, but also with calves, lambs, baby yaks, even full-grown pregnant sheep. Ordinarily quite comfortable because of the open fire, the *yurt* can become even warmer due to the breathing and the body heat of half a dozen human beings and as many animals. It is so comfortable and warm inside a *yurt* on such a night that it is the custom to sleep naked on piles of clothing and furs, although fur coats are used for covers when strong winds find their way through the seams of the felt and drop the temperatures inside to an uncomfortable level.

In the agricultural cooperatives, *yurts* appear side by side with new one-story wooden or brick buildings with sheet-iron roofs. Farther north, in the vicinity of the Siberian border, Mongolian houses strongly resemble village houses of the Russian type with wooden roofs. In the cities and towns, apartments are becoming available in increasing numbers to agricultural and factory workers. How much progress has been achieved in this area can be seen from the available figures. Only 340 new apartments were built during the first five-year plan; 2,000 were constructed during the second five-year plan, which added a total of more than 112 million square feet to the living quarters of city dwellers. Almost three times this amount of additional living space was added during the years from 1948 to 1960.

Nearly all these new apartments have been built with assistance from other Communist countries. During 1956–60, the Soviet Union constructed apartment houses in Ulan Bator, adding more than 43 million square feet of living space, and at a time when relations between Mongolia and Communist China were amicable, China contributed about 54 million square feet of housing construction in Ulan Bator. Czechoslovakia also has helped Mongolia in its program of modern housing construction.

The Mongols, who depend chiefly on their cattle and sheep for food, have a diet consisting mostly of meat and milk products. They consume large quantities of tea, but tea, as the Mongols make it, is a food rather than a drink. Mongolian tea is prepared by brewing Chinese green tea, to which is added a large quantity of fresh milk, salt, and butter or, quite often, mutton fat. Since salt is used instead of sugar, this concoction tastes more like a tea-soup than like regular tea.

When a guest is received in a Mongolian household, he is offered tea to drink while the mutton is being cooked. The mutton is served in large slices, which taste different from mutton in Western countries because the Mongols use little, if any, salt. The meat course is followed by a broth, and the meal is concluded with *kumys*—fermented mare's milk, the most famous drink of the Mongols.

The national article of dress is the *deli,* a long robelike gown. It is folded over left to right and is tied with a long cloth belt that goes several times about the waist. *Delis* for ordinary wear are made of plain cotton material. For holidays, Mongols wear *delis* made of silk. *Delis* worn on cold winter days are woven of heavy woolen material and often have a lining of white lamb's fur. Mongolian boots have thick soles and turned-up toes. Mongolian city-dwellers, however, have largely switched to Western-type clothing, and very seldom does one find Mongolian boots in Ulan Bator.

The average family in Mongolia has never been large. At the time of the 1918 census, there were slightly more than half a million people in the country living in 125,000 *yurts,* which means that the average family consisted of just over four persons. The small size of the average family was due in large measure to the high infant mortality rate and the short life expectancy of the children and adults that survived. The principal scourge of children in Mongolia has always been gastric troubles, particularly diarrhea and dysentery, which account for the majority of deaths among the young, although eye and skin diseases are also prevalent.

Much of the ill health among the Mongols in former

days resulted from the incredible filth in which they lived. Mongolian nomads, as a rule, detested water and never washed their bodies during their entire life, except for an occasional sprinkling of water on hands or face. Dishes in the typical *yurt* were never washed. Clothing was simple, so simple in fact that both men and women wore clothing of the same crude design made from the same fabric. There was no underwear, just a shirt and baggy pants over which a long robe was customarily worn, reaching to the ankles, with sleeves that extended 6 to 8 inches beyond the fingertips. In winter, heavy sheepskin coats were worn and warm peaked hats of fur. Soft felt stockings and soft leather boots with soft felt soles protected the feet. Clothing was seldom if ever washed and was worn until it rotted or fell away in rags.

In the days when nearly all Mongols were nomads, practically all adults suffered from piles as a result of constant daily horseback riding. Cancer of the stomach was a quite common cause of death. Other fatal stomach disorders could be traced to the diet, which lacked variety. Indeed, the only variety was that which occurred between the summer months, when the diet depended heavily on the consumption of milk and milk products, and the winter months, when there was a shortage of milk and the Mongols ate meat, usually only once a day. The meat was usually mutton, occasionally horsemeat or the meat of camels or other domestic animals. The meat of animals that had succumbed to disease was eaten. Fish and fowl were considered by the Mongols to be unclean food. Under such conditions, the high mortality rate of prerevolutionary Mongolia is not at all surprising. Improved living standards since the revolution reflect the health services provided to the population of Mongolia during the last few decades. Fifty years ago, health care was provided by lamas, whose treatments were based, as a rule, on superstition. There were no hospitals in Mongolia and no doctors until 1924, when the first Russian medical personnel came at the request of the Mongolian government. Hospital facilities were eventually provided; by 1940, there were 17 hospitals and 150 health units throughout the country. A school for limited training of medical personnel had been opened in 1931, but it was not until 1947 that the first group of medical doctors was graduated from the School of Medicine of the Mongolian State University. Ever since then, the number of doctors, nurses, doctor's aides, hospitals, and hospital beds has been steadily growing. In 1968, five hundred physicians were graduated, and more attention was being paid to the necessity of supplying doctors and doctor's aides to rural areas that previously had lacked medical assistance. Each *aymag* has at least one hospital, and every agricultural cooperative and state farm has a health unit, served by a doctor or medical assistant. Plague, smallpox, and other contagious diseases that formerly killed thousands of Mongols each year have been eliminated. The death rate of children has been steadily decreasing; in 1961, it was one-seventh of what it had been in 1958.

Similarly impressive progress has been made in education. When Mongolia proclaimed its independence in 1921, most of the population was illiterate. Formal education was practically nonexistent. In the early years of the twentieth century, there was only one secular school in the country and that was in the capital and served a very small part of the population. The main educational facilities were in the monasteries, which concentrated on the study of religious literature, primarily in the Tibetan language.

By 1963, the number of schools in Mongolia had increased to five hundred, which was 35 times more schools than there had been in 1924, three years after independence had been declared. By the end of the 1960's, there were more than six hundred elementary and high schools, including 104 evening schools for general education, and the total number of students attending schools of all types exceeded 248,000.

Partly responsible for this rapid development is the two-tier system of education introduced in 1955, which makes compulsory an elementary education for the entire population and a seven-year education for children living in Ulan Bator. Illiterate adults are given an opportunity to learn to read and write in special evening schools. Although the majority of children entering elementary school never finish high school, the number of high school graduates is very impressive in a country that was almost 100 per cent illiterate fifty years ago. Recent figures show that 66 out of every 1,000 Mongols have completed a high school or college education.

The reduction of illiteracy can be attributed, to a large extent, to the change-over from the old Mongolian script to the new alphabet introduced in 1945. The results were immediate and startling. In 1940, 90 per cent of all the people in Mongolia were illiterate. Five years after the introduction of the new alphabet, the number was down to 35 per cent of the population. By now, illiteracy has been nearly eliminated. The few remaining illiterates are almost entirely among the very old.

The Soviet Union was of great assistance in Mongolia's efforts to wipe out illiteracy. In the 1930's, Russian educators were sent to Mongolia to initiate extensive education programs, and many young men and women were sent from Mongolia to study in Russian universities. The rapid increase in the number of elementary and high schools in the 1940's demanded a corresponding increase in the number of teachers and an increase in the years of schooling that went into the training of each teacher. Before 1952, there were almost a thousand teachers in Mongolia who had either completed high school or who had had teacher training in high school, but there were no teachers who had ever been to college. By 1960, 1,247 of the 4,118 persons engaged in teaching either had completed college or had had some college education.

The beginnings of higher education in Mongolia can be traced to the need for teacher training and the establishment in 1940 of an Institute for Teacher Improvement, with classes conducted at night. The following year, the Higher School of Party Education was opened in Ulan Bator, and the year after that the doors of the Mongolian State University were opened in Ulan Bator with the assistance of personnel from the University of Moscow. In its first year of existence, the new university had ninety-five students. Twenty years later, the number of students had grown to about two thousand, and some departments of the university had developed to such an extent that they were reorganized as independent institutions. The School of Agriculture of the State University became the independent Institute of Agriculture in 1958. The School of Economics is now an independent institute, and in 1957 the former Institute for Teacher Improvement became the State Pedagogical Institute, a four-year college.

Today there are in all of Mongolia six institutions of higher learning, including the State University at Ulan Bator. The professional schools and the institutions of higher learning graduated five hundred specialists altogether in 1967. This is not an insignificant number in view of the small size of the population as a whole, and in an area the size of Mongolia every graduate is an asset of great value to the economic and industrial development of the country. In addition to elementary and high schools for general education, Mongolia has a number of schools for professional training, where technicians and specialists in various trades are trained for four-year periods. There are eighteen of these professional schools. The level of professional training in such schools is higher than that in U.S. vocational high schools, being more nearly comparable to junior college standards, except that the stress is on engineering and technical subjects, rather than general education. There are numerous other technical and vocational schools in which the training is on a level comparable to that received in a U.S. high school.

The gradual increase in the number of people entering schools of higher education inevitably led to a general improvement in the level of scientific inquiry and research throughout the Mongolian People's Republic. The number of scientists steadily increased until the government decided that the time was ripe for the creation of a Mongolian Academy of Sciences. This occurred in May, 1961, when the former Committee on Science and Higher Education was renamed the Academy of Sciences and entrusted with the study of Mongolia, its natural resources, and other areas of importance to its survival as an independent state in today's rapidly expanding world of technology. There were originally five research institutes in the Academy. Now there are ten, in such fields as animal husbandry and agriculture, physics and chemistry, geography, the study of permafrost, geology, biology, medicine, economics, history, and language.

The Academy boasts a good observatory, an adequate library of scientific literature, its own publishing house for issuing scientific works in the Mongolian language, and several supplementary establishments, including agricultural experimental stations, which are actively engaged in the development of irrigation.

At the present time, the Mongolian Academy of Sciences is staffed by ten academicians and twenty-seven corresponding members. It is far behind similar organizations in Russia and the more advanced countries in the rest of the world, but in view of its initial handicaps—the shortage of Mongols with a college education and the comparatively recent ending of illiteracy—the accomplishments of the Academy are commendable. It has attained a rather high level of scholastic achievement in a remarkably short period of time.

From earliest times, religion has played an important role in the cultural development of Mongolia. The Mongols in the west practiced a form of shamanism but later adopted Islam. The Mongols in the east turned to Buddhism, which had been brought into the country from Tibet as early as the sixth century and was widely practiced in the days of Genghis Khan. Not until the sixteenth and seventeenth centuries, when Buddhism gradually assumed the form now known as Lamaism, was any one religion dominant in Mongolia.

One significant feature of the Buddhist religion that was

carried over into Lamaism was the part played by the Lamaist monasteries as carriers of culture. Lamaist monasteries, like European monasteries, were important centers of cultural life and eventually played an important role in the economic and political life of the country. It was customary for each family to send at least one son to a monastery to become a member of the ever growing class of monks, or lamas as they were called in Mongolia. Great influence was exerted by the celibate lamas on the national social structure, and their numbers increased to such an extent that population growth was seriously affected. In 1918, for instance, only three years before the Communists took over the country, there were seven hundred monasteries in Mongolia and a hundred thousand lamas. In other words, from one-fifth to one-sixth of the total population was celibate males.

The energetic efforts of the Communist rulers of Mongolia to destroy religion can be seen in the fact that the lamas have practically disappeared from the scene. The lower ranks within the monastic social structure joined the workers or became members of the peasant classes. Lamas higher in the hierarchy either left the country or were accused of revolutionary activities and were liquidated. By 1940, monasteries in Mongolia had ceased to function as monasteries. Wooden or brick monastery buildings were dismantled, and the materials were used for the construction of dwellings or office buildings. Most of the surviving monasteries are preserved as monuments of Mongolian architecture and, like many former places of worship in the Soviet Union, are used as museums. Among these are the famous monastery of Choydzhin-Lama and the no less famous Erdeni-Tsu monastery, located about 280 miles south of Ulan Bator in the wide valley of the Orkhon River. The latter monastery is considered to be the first ever built in Mongolia. It was constructed in 1586 on the site of Karakorum, the ancient capital of Genghis Khan. Architecturally, it is a mixture of several styles, Mongolian, Tibetan, and Chinese.

The influence of the Lamaist religion on the lives of the Mongols has been thoroughly undermined, if not completely destroyed. A few elderly Mongols continue to worship in the old way in the Gandan Tekchinling monastery in the north-western part of the city of Ulan Bator. This is the sole surviving monastery still used for religious purposes. Within its confines, eighty-two lamas remain, but they are as old if not older than the surviving worshippers. These seem to be the last remnants of Lamaism in Mongolia. It is, of course, impossible to estimate the number of Mongolians who have religious beliefs. Many undoubtedly conceal their religious feelings for reasons of personal safety.

For many years the population of Mongolia decreased, but now the population increases between 2.5 and 3 per cent a year. The improved health measures and a marked decrease in the number of celibate lamas are in part responsible for this development. Another reason for the increase in the population of Mongolia has been encouragement by the state of larger families. In contrast to many countries, in which the dangers of the population explosion are so acute that birth control and abortion have been introduced and legalized, mothers of large families in Mongolia are given monetary awards and medals. More than 40 million *tugriks* were given to such mothers between 1949 and 1959. Those with exceptionally large families are awarded Mothers' Glory medals. In two years (1958 and 1959) almost three thousand mothers with exceptionally large families were given Mothers' Glory medals, first grade, and about twenty-four thousand received Mothers' Glory, second grade. These medal-winning mothers received state subsidies amounting to almost 3 million *tugriks*.

The result of these measures has been that the population of Mongolia almost doubled in the forty-five years between 1918 and 1963 (from 542,600 to 1,018,900). This is equivalent to a population density of 0.9 persons per square mile in 1918 and 1.72 persons per square mile in 1963.

The corresponding decrease in the death rate that has accompanied the rising birth rate has aided greatly in increasing the natural growth rate. In the 1955–67 period, for instance, the number of births increased from 32.3 per thousand persons to 39.6; at the same time, the number of deaths per thousand decreased from 14.2 to 9.7. This combination of factors resulted in an increase of more than 75 per cent in the so-called natural growth rate (from 18.1 per thousand persons to 32.7).

The growth in population has naturally resulted in significant changes in the age structure of Mongolian society during the last few decades. Modern Mongolia can be classified as a country of youth. In 1965, young people 18 years old and under comprised no less than 45 per cent of the entire population, and the 35-and-under group represented 68 per cent of all the people of the nation. Due to the rapid increase in life expectancy (51 years in 1940, 56 years in 1956, and 64 years in 1963), the number of people above the age of 45 has also been on the increase. This age group now accounts for 20 per cent of the total population.

Another significant factor in the overall population picture is the increase in the number of women over men. In 1956, the census in Mongolia showed that there were 425,200 women and 420,500 men; this excess of women over men has been a decisive factor in the composition of the labor force. More than 41 per cent of the workers in industry and 52.2 per cent of all workers in the rural economy are women. Women constitute 70 per cent of all workers in the Ministry of Health, 30 per cent of all teachers and students in institutions of higher learning, and 32 per cent of all workers in the arts. Almost 22 per cent of the elected members of the *Khural* are women, and over 20 per cent of those elected to the local *khurals* are women.

13 The Arts and Recreation

Written Mongolian has two forms. The most widely used today is that of the modern literary language, based principally on the language spoken by the Khalkha Mongols and using the Cyrillic form of writing adopted in 1945. The original, or classical, form of written Mongolian first appeared at about the end of the twelfth century. Three well-defined periods in the development of the ancient written language can be established. During the first period, which lasted for about a hundred years, written Mongolian was used mainly for administrative purposes. During the second period (the fourteenth, fifteenth, and sixteenth centuries), the written language, still used for official correspondence and other administrative purposes, was used for translating Buddhist literature. Most of the translations were made from the Tibetan language, and many words from it became part of Mongolian.

The third period, which lasted from about 1600 to 1945, is the most important. Many old words and grammar forms, which had become difficult to recognize and whose meanings had become obscure, were discarded, and many new words were borrowed, especially from the Tibetan. The ancient Uigur alphabet, which had been used since earliest

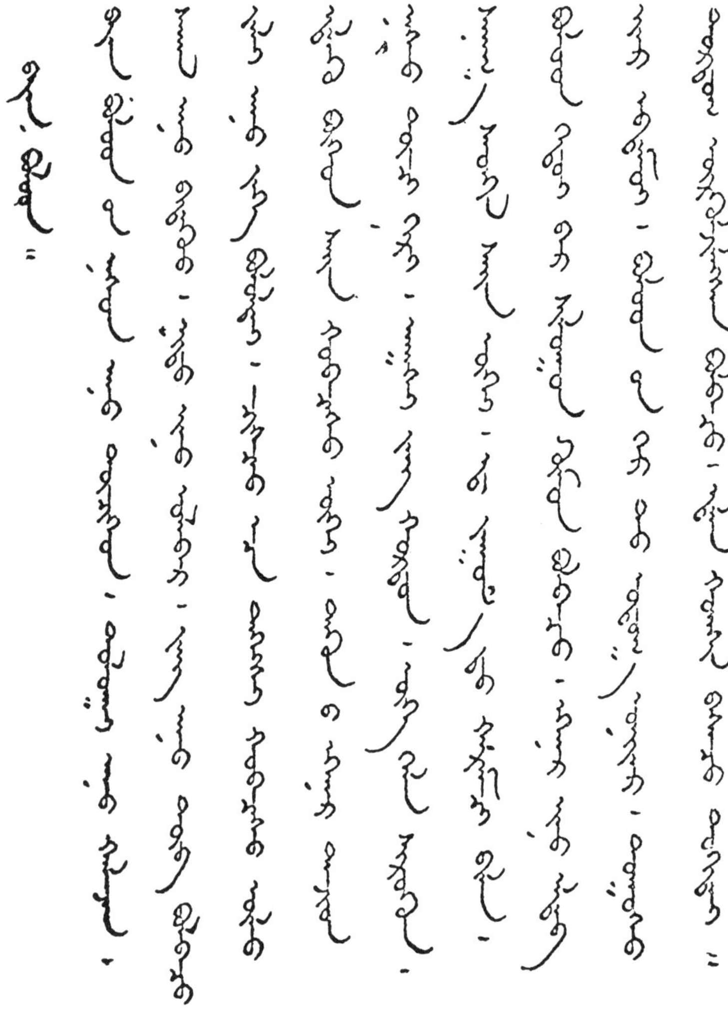

Fig. 1. The Classical Mongolian Script

times, gradually changed into the classical Mongolian alphabet.

Classical Mongolian consists of twenty basic letters, representing the principal Mongolian speech sounds, and eight additional letters, representing sounds absorbed into Mongolian from foreign languages. Writing using the classical alphabet (Fig. 1) was vertical, read from top to bottom and from right to left, as in the Chinese style of writing. This form of writing is still in use in the Inner Mongolian Autonomous Region of China, but in 1945 it was superseded in the Mongolian People's Republic by a new form of writing based on the Cyrillic alphabet, common to Russia, Yugoslavia, and Bulgaria. The reason for the change-over was simplification. The new alphabet consists of thirty-three letters from the modern Cyrillic alphabet plus two additional characters that represent sounds of spoken Mongolian not otherwise reproducible. The modern Mongolian alphabet (Fig. 2), then, consists of thirty-five characters—thirty-three capital and lower-case letters and two without capitals.

Аа, Бб, Вв, Гг, Дд, Ее, Ёё, Жж, Зз, Ии, Йй, Кк, Лл, Мм, Нн, Оо, Өө, Пп, Рр, Сс, Тт, Уу, Үү, Фф, Хх, Цц, Чч, Шш, Щщ, ъ, ы, ь, Ээ, Юю, Яя.

Fig. 2. The Modern Mongolian Alphabet

Fifty years ago Mongolia could not boast of a single publication. Not until 1924 did the first newspaper make its appearance. By 1940, there were six newspapers and eight journals printed in classical Mongolian. Twenty-five years later the country could boast of thirty newspapers and twenty journals. The most popular of these is the newspaper *Unen* (Truth), which, like *Pravda,* is the official publication of the government and party. Today, all appear in modern Mongolian script.

Publication is not limited to periodicals and newspapers. The Mongolian State Publishing House in Ulan Bator prints books in the Mongolian, Russian, Kazakh, and Chinese languages. In a single year, this publishing house printed almost 11 million copies of 952 separate books and brochures, evidence that Mongolia is forging ahead in its program of education by introducing the printed word to the masses. Much that is published is propaganda translated from the Russian. It is not surprising that the most popular authors in Mongolia are Lenin and Marx, judging from the quantities of their works translated and distributed. Readers outside Mongolia are able to read Mongolian literature in translation. In addition to the languages mentioned above, the State Publishing House prints Mongolian works in English, French, and German for distribution to more than thirty foreign countries.

Until recent times, Mongolia had no written literature. There was a strong oral tradition, and folklore and legends were passed on from person to person and from generation to generation. In modern times, a group of young writers made their appearance, and modern Mongolian literature was born. The two most prominent writers of this early period were D. Natsagdorj and Ts. Damdinsuren. Their lot as trail-blazers was not easy. As in most Communist countries, Mongolian writers were required to conform to regulations regarding what they could write. They were particularly restricted in their choice of plots and in their depiction of heroes and heroines. This was especially true during the time that Russia was ruled by Stalin. Since Stalin's death, restrictions have eased somewhat. At one of the sessions of the Third Congress of Mongolian Writers in 1962, D. Tomor Ochir, secretary of the party's central committee, said: "During the period of the personality cult, our literature was forced to minimize the leadership of the party and the creativeness of the Mongolian people, to distort reality, to sing the praises of individuals, and to carry out indiscriminate, dogmatic criticism. This destroyed the ability of literature to assert a positive influence on the minds of the people and helped promote a type of writing that has nothing to do with reality." The key phrase "forced to minimize the leadership of the party" indicates that Mongolian writers cannot write freely. Nevertheless, this speech was instrumental in easing the pressures, and writers are now permitted to be more creative than they could be before the speech was made.

Much of present-day Mongolian literature is devoted to the "education" of the people, particularly the young. This is the primary role that has been assigned to literature in Mongolia. That this education is still slanted can be seen in another passage from Ochir's statement: "Our writers, through their writings, have the privilege and the job of educating the people to be new members of our newly built socialist society, to respect each other, to develop their minds to cope with their responsibilities, and to love labor. . . . The Fourteenth Congress of the Mongolian Peoples' Revolutionary Party has called upon Mongolian writers to give a true and attractive portrayal of our hard-working, heroic, honest people. . . . Young writers represent the new generation. They are the future masters of their own fate. They must learn how to influence the minds of young children and how to teach youth to love their country, to respect labor, and to be loyal to the principle of socialism and Communism."

The literature of modern Mongolia has two recurrent themes: the recent revolutionary past and life as it is lived in the country at the present time. Novels are popular, and short stories have been a mainstay of the new literature from the beginning. The founder of the modern school of writers is D. Natsagdorj, whose best-known works are *Son of the Old World, New Year,* and *Bitter Tears.* Another well-liked storyteller is Ts. Damdinsuren, author of *Spurned Girl* and *On the Altay.* New books by younger writers are constantly appearing. Some of the more popular titles of recent years are *The Transparent Tamir* by Ch. Lodoidamba, *Turbulent Time* by D. Namdag, and *Khalkhyn-Gol* and *Sorrows and Joys* by U. Ulambayar.

The Mongolian theater, like the literature of Mongolia, has undergone a change since 1962, when it emerged from the regimented, repressive atmosphere that marked the early days of its existence. The history of the national theater goes back to 1930, the year in which Soviet experts in theater arts opened an academy where young Mongols were given two-year courses in acting and in ballet. The following year, the first state theater was opened in Ulan Bator. Later renamed the State Theater of Opera and Ballet, it presented performances that were completely new forms of artistic expression to the Mongols. The number of theaters has grown steadily, as has the number of people who attend concerts, plays, and ballets. There are now six professional and sixteen semiprofessional theaters, in which hundreds of performers take part in drama, folk singing, folk dancing, opera, and ballet.

The fact that organized theater is so young in Mongolia does not mean that the Mongols had no entertainment until it was established. Ritual dances and music are centuries old. Singing is characterized by the continuous wailing sound and is usually accompanied by musical instruments, some of the violin variety and others of the guitar and mandolin families.

Folk dancing, particularly during holiday celebrations, has played an important role in the life of the Mongols since time immemorial. One of the most famous of the folk dances is the *Bielgee* (Dance of the Body), whose origins can be traced into the distant past when, according to legend, the Manchu conquerors forbade the local people to assemble in large groups in public places, fearing that in such large gatherings a single spark—such as an inspiring speech— might lead to a spontaneous rebellion. The result of these prohibitions was that dances formerly performed out doors came to be performed in the narrow confines of the *yurts*. Leg-room was at a premium in the circular felt-covered tents, so the popular native dance used the parts of the body that require little space for rhythmic movement, the hands and head.

In the old days, the *Bielgee* was usually performed by a slim and graceful girl, accompanied by one of the traditional Mongolian musical instruments, such as the *morin-khuur* or the *tovshur*. In modern times, however, this still-popular dance is most often performed on the stage, usually by a group of dancers who compete with each other in the complicated gyrations of the dance. The *Bielgee* is a staple in the repertoire of the Folk Song and Dance ensemble of the Mongolian People's Republic. Nerguy, a soloist of the ensemble, was awarded a silver medal for her performance of this native dance at the International Festival in Helsinki, Finland.

Ballet has recently become popular in Mongolia. A great improvement in the national ballet has been noticed since the return to Mongolia of more than thirty dancers who received their training in the Soviet ballet schools in Perm and Tashkent. These young dancers have become the nucleus of a new ballet theater.

A somewhat more traditional form of entertainment is the Mongolian puppet show, which, originally, was devoted almost exclusively to portraying scenes from Buddhist mythology. The most important ingredient that goes into the manufacture of the gaily painted puppets is goat's fat.

The movie industry was introduced into Mongolia in 1936 and quickly made itself an important part of the cultural life of the country. The first films were made with the assistance of Soviet film-makers, but the industry is apparently now on its own, with several all-Mongolian films to its credit. Mongolkino, the Mongolian equivalent of Hollywood, releases four feature films, twenty-four documentaries, and twenty-four newsreels a year. Considering that this huge nation, with its small population thinly spread over its vast steppes and rugged mountains, is a latecomer to movie-making as it is to most other manifestations of modern culture, this film output is quite impressive. To meet the growing demand for films, however, foreign films must be imported. Most of them come from the Soviet Union.

Tremendous strides have been made in the quality of Mongolkino's productions over three decades. *Modern Mongolia,* a documentary filmed in color, was awarded a prize

at the film festival in Karlovy Vary, Czechoslovakia, and
another all-Mongolian film, *On the Doorstep of Life,* was
enthusiastically received at the Asian and African film
festival in Tashkent in Soviet Central Asia in 1958. The
country has its own film stars. Tsevelsuren, an actress well-
known to Mongolian movie fans, won a silver-medal award
at the International Movie Festival in Moscow in 1959 for
her best performance (in the leading feminine role category)
in the Mongolkino production *Messenger of the People.*

The Russians introduced the circus to Mongolia. The first
circus, organized in 1941, was patterned faithfully after the
world-famous circus of the Soviet Union and remains one
of the most popular forms of entertainment in Mongolia.

The performance of operas by the State Theater of Opera
and Ballet has been greatly influenced by Mongolian adapta-
tions of Russian operas, among which Tchaikovsky's *Eugene
Onegin,* based on Pushkin's famous poem, and Alexander
Dargomizhsky's *Russalka* (The Mermaid) are favorites. Of
equal interest, however, are operas by Mongolian composers,
such as *Princess Dolgor and Arat Damdin,* which incorpor-
ates traditional folk melodies in its score. The most popular
Mongolian opera, *Three Sad Hills,* also utilizes folk tunes. It
was the first Mongolian opera to be presented to the public
when the State Theater began operation in Ulan Bator in the
1930's. Originally, it had a rather primitive plot, but its li-
bretto has undergone several revisions. In 1942, it was staged
as a completely new production with a revised score by the
young composer Damdinsuren and has been presented every
season since.

Painting and sculpture have not been neglected in modern
Mongolia. More than 140 Mongolian artists participated in

the Mongolian Art Exhibition of 1967. Four hundred paintings, sculptures, and other art objects were exhibited. Two styles were apparent in the paintings—the European representational style and the traditional Mongolian style, which is distinguished by bright colors and an Oriental lack of perspective. Most of the paintings hung in the exhibit contained an ideological message. The subjects reflected the Communist tendency to idealize life on collective farms, in the factories, and in the mines. "Moving to a New Place" by Minjur shows a cattle breeder's family moving cattle and possessions to a new summer pasture. U. Yadamsuren's "Friendship" delivers a lofty ideological message, and a historical moment is recaptured in O. Mayagmar's painting, which depicts the Baron Ungern von Sternberg at the moment of his capture.

Sports, particularly archery and horseback riding, have always been important to the Mongols. A third competitive sport, the native form of wrestling, developed as a ritualistic exercise. Among the sports introduced into the country in modern times, the most popular are track and field athletics, gymnastics, bicycle racing, volleyball, basketball, skiing, skating, soccer, Ping-Pong, and mountain climbing.

As a rule, sports activities are regulated and supervised by the twenty-four athletic societies, whose combined membership includes eighty-two thousand young Mongols. From the standpoint of sports, the country can be said to have come of age in 1964, when Mongolian athletes participated in the Olympic Games for the first time.

The traditional sports of Mongolia have always been in evidence during national holidays, particularly during *Nadom*. Formerly, *Nadom* was a regional holiday celebrating the anniversary of an important event such as the birth of an heir to a title or the day the ruling prince came of age. *Nadom* was partly a religious ritual, and the best wrestlers, archers, and horseback riders were selected by the prince to be in his retinue and to take part in countrywide athletic contests. *Nadoms* usually took place in the summer, when the horses were well fed and had received ample training, and when there were sufficient supplies of dairy products, particularly the beverage made from fermented mare's milk (*kumys*).

When the Communists came to power in Mongolia, they did not eliminate the *Nadoms,* but there is no longer any religious element in the celebrations. National *Nadom,* which begins on July 11 as a national holiday and usually lasts several days, now celebrates the anniversary of the revolution that brought the Communists to power. The *Nadom* usually begins with a parade of the participants, who pass a platform occupied by the members of the presidium of the *Khural.* The sporting events that take place in the stadium in Ulan Bator, which has a capacity of 15,000 spectators, include the new sports as well as the traditional wrestling, archery, and horseback riding.

Wrestling is usually the first event. Competing wrestlers, who have been preparing for the great event for many months, study each other attentively, waiting for the appropriate moment to make a sudden leap that will throw the opponent off balance. The first man to fall to the ground is the loser. Wrestlers with five wins are awarded honorary titles. Those who win five or six matches receive the title of Falcon. Those who win from seven to nine matches are designated Elephants. Wrestlers who triumph ten or eleven times receive the highly coveted title of Lion. A Lion who is awarded the title twice becomes a Titan. If he wins the title once more, he becomes an All-People's Titan, and a fourth such victory makes him Invincible. No matter how many times a wrestler wins the title of Lion after that, he remains an All-People's Invincible Titan for the rest of his life without having to take part in the wrestling matches at future *Nadoms*.

Archery is as popular as wrestling. Ancient Chinese chronicles state that the Mongols practiced the art of archery as far back as the sixth century, at which time the Mongols were accustomed to hunt hares with bows and arrows while riding horseback at full speed. Most Mongols are trained in archery from early childhood and are excellent archers. The competitions held in the stadium at Ulan Bator during the National *Nadom* are conducted in three rounds. Each competitor is given twenty arrows. Four are used in the first round, which is comparatively easy. In the second round, archers use eight arrows and aim at targets with values of from 2 to 30 points each. In the third and most difficult round, the archers use the same targets but stand with their backs to the targets and at a given signal turn and let fly in an archer's equivalent of an American "quick draw" contest. The last eight arrows are graded as in the second round, and the archer who chalks up the most points receives the title of Sharpshooter.

The last of the three traditional sporting events that dominate the National *Nadom* is horse racing. The best and fastest horses available are selected and trained months in advance. Their diet is closely regulated, and they are grazed on the best grazing lands available. The most unusual feature of the traditional Mongolian horse race is that only children, ranging in age from five to twelve, are permitted to participate. Most Mongolian children are accomplished horseback riders almost from their diaper days. As a result, the grueling fifteen-mile race is an exciting event both for the adults and the youth of the nation. The victorious rider is rewarded with a cup of *kumys* and so is the steed, but the heady beverage is merely sprinkled over the head and back of the winning horse.

Mongolia has been the home of a large variety of animals since prehistoric times. The forests of northern and northwestern Mongolia have an abundance of brown bears, elks, wild birds, foxes, and squirrels. The prairie lands abound in wildcats, tarbagans, and prairie wolves. The hunting of wild animals has become so intensive that many species have been threatened with extinction, and the Mongolian government is taking measures to protect them. The most famous of the protected animals are the Przhevalsky horses, first discovered in the second half of the nineteenth century by the Russian explorer after whom they were named. Another protected species is the Gobi bear.

The hunting of wild animals is mainly for the purpose of obtaining furs and food, but the hunting of the wolf is a matter of honor with the Mongols. The wolf is widespread throughout Mongolia. It is the scourge of the herdsmen. It kills more cattle, horses, and sheep than any other wild animal does and occasionally threatens bodily harm to humans. The hunting of the wolf has only one purpose—to destroy as many of these predatory animals as possible.

Each region has its own type of wolf hunt, conducted either by individual hunters or by all the *arats* of the settlement. Winter and spring are the prime wolf-hunting seasons. Long experience has taught the Mongols that the most efficient way to kill the largest number of animals is to seek them out in packs. An attempt is made to wound one of the animals in the pack. If the wolf is not killed, the other animals in the pack will attack it and tear it to pieces. While the other wolves are engrossed in this bloody business, the hunters seize the opportunity to shoot and kill as many of them as possible. If the first wolf is killed instantly, the rest of the pack disperses, and there is only one victim.

Wolf-hunting with whips has developed into a sport in the Gobi region, where the use of guns for hunting is looked down on. When a Mongol on horseback detects a lone wolf on the steppe, he chases the animal. When the distance between hunter and prey is so short that the wolf senses it will be overtaken, it will generally turn around and attack the hunter. At this critical moment, the Mongol swings his whip and, if his aim is good, hits the animal between the eyes with the end of the whip, to which is attached a piece of lead. One blow with this powerful weapon, when properly administered, is sufficient to kill a wolf, but the utmost agility on the part of horse and rider is required.

Another form of hunting highly developed in Mongolia is falconry, but eagles instead of falcons are used. Hunting with eagles is particularly popular with the Kazakhs in the western part of the country. Eagles are expert hunters; they will not only spot and attack small animals such as hares and foxes but will on occasion attack young wolves. Good hunting eagles are not easy to obtain. The best are those that are captured in the nest before they have learned to fly and are trained to fly only when released by their keepers. Obtaining the birds is dangerous, not only because of the inaccessibility of the nests, which are found in some of the most mountainous regions of Mongolia, but also because of the fierce, protective instincts of the female eagle, who will go to any length to protect her offspring. Training usually takes two years.

The animals most prized for their skins in Mongolia are tarbagans, whose furs are of great commercial value. They are usually found in the steppes, where they live in underground nests in large colonies. Many ways have been developed to entice these small animals from their underground shelters. One method requires that the hunter wear a white robe. Why a white-robed hunter attracts the curiosity of tarbagans more than a hunter in ordinary garb does is not clear, but the fact remains that they are intensely interested in men clothed in white and a sudden stop or change of gait lures them out of their holes.

Tarbagan-hunters must be excellent marksmen because the animals are usually shot when the hunter is from 80 to 100 feet away. If a perfect skin is to be obtained, the animal must be shot in the ear. More than 1 million tarbagan skins are obtained by hunters in Mongolia each year. The Mongols are partial to the meat, which is tender and tastes somewhat like pork. Tarbagan fat is a valuable by-product. It resembles the fat of seals in that it will not freeze, even in the coldest Mongolian weather.

The Mongolian People's Republic and neighboring Inner Mongolia contain some of the world's best hunting grounds for skeletons of dinosaurs and other extinct beasts. In sands of the Gobi, archeologists and zoologists have found bones of animals that became extinct millions of years ago.

14 Vanishing Customs

Mongolia has undergone tremendous social and economic changes in the last fifty years, particularly in the cities, where manifestations of modern civilization are gradually superseding the nomadic way of life. However, in present-day Mongolia, some aspects of old Mongolia remain.

Before the revolution of 1921, Mongolian society was divided into five clearly defined classes: (1) the princes, (2) the nobility, (3) the lamas, or priestly class, (4) the "free" peasants, and (5) the serfs.

The ruling class—the princes—was the smallest in number. Each *khoshun* (principality) was ruled by a hereditary prince. Because the title could be transferred only from the father to the eldest son, the number of princes remained unchanged. At the time the new order was proclaimed in 1921, there were only 115 princes in all Mongolia. Each member of this highly exclusive group proudly claimed to be descended from the first great khan, Genghis Khan.

The second most privileged class was *taijai* (members of the untitled nobility), composed mostly of the younger offspring of the princely families, who were unable to inherit the title and office of prince but who were entitled by birth to the status of nobility. The word *taijai,* of Chinese origin, apparently was introduced into Mongolia with the installation of Manchu rule in the seventeenth century. According to the census of 1918, there were 13,274 nobles out of a total male population of a quarter of a million. The princes and nobles together accounted for between 5 and 6 per cent of the entire male population before the revolution.

The largest single class was the lamas. At the time of the 1918 census, there were 115,000 lamas in Mongolia, between 40 and 45 per cent of the total male population. In prerevolutionary days, Mongolia was a theocracy, and the priestly class was the most powerful of the five classes. (Only in the four major *aymags* and in the smaller *khoshuns* was power relegated to the hereditary princes.) Since the sixteenth century, the lamas had been the chief propagators of Lamaism, known as the "religion of the yellow hats" from the colorful headgear worn by the priests. As spiritual rulers of the Mongols, the lamas exerted a tremendous influence on the life of the country, but this influence was due not only to their role as spiritual rulers but also to the fact that there were so many of them.

The life of a Lama was economically unproductive, but it was not idle. A boy was inducted into the society of lamas at the age of 7 or 8 years. He was sent to a monastery to live with a lama tutor, whom he would serve, and to learn about the Lamaist religion. In addition to menial tasks, he was required to study Tibetan prayer books and other literature concerned with the religious life and to learn the Lamaist catechism. This elementary step to becoming a full-fledged lama occupied the novice for the seven or eight years until he reached the age of 15.

The next period was spent in a secondary school or seminary, where a more thorough interpretation of prayers was taught, together with the simpler aspects of religious dogma and Lamaist philosophy. At the age of 25, the student graduated into the third and formal stage of religious training, which was conducted in one of the theological academies. There he was introduced to the higher religious mysteries, a process that continued for twenty years. Upon graduating, at the age of 45, the title of *gabji* (doctor of theology) was bestowed on the lama.

The learning process never ended for the lamas. The fourth stage of education began upon graduation. This was a more relaxed form of study and voluntary research into a specialized subject related to philosophy or theology. If the lama was fortunate, he might be awarded the highest scholastic title, *agrimba*. That this elevated state was not easy to attain can be seen from the fact that of the 115,000 lamas included in the 1918 census, only about fifty were *agrimbas*.

Because the lamas were the only literate class, the Lamaist monasteries became the centers of the cultural as well as religious life of the country. Nearly every *khoshun* had at least one monastery. Not all lamas lived within the confines of the monasteries, however. About two-thirds of them lived in isolated regions as hermits and holy men. Still others settled in populated areas, where some acquired families despite their pledge of celibacy.

Below the class of the lamas were two peasant classes—the free peasants and the serfs. The free peasants bore the major burden of taxation but were their own masters. Serfs were peasants who had not achieved freedom from masters and who had little chance of doing so.

The lot of the peasant, "free" or otherwise, was pitiful, but the lot of the serfs was the worst of all. The serf was the property of the nobility and could be used as a household servant or in way the master pleased. He could be beaten, and he could never move away without his master's permission. He could be bought and sold. He could be given away as a present or gambled away. Serfs not required to give personal or household service to their noble lords led a typically nomadic life, tending their lord's herds and following the animals in their seasonal migrations.

At first, serfs were the exclusive property of the princes and the nobility, but as the church gained influence, high lamas and eventually monasteries became owners of serfs. By the beginning of the twentieth century, three classes of serfs could be identified: the *khamjilga,* property of the princes; the *albatu,* property of the nobility; and the *shabinar,* property of the monasteries and the high-ranking lamas.

The *albatus* and free peasants were the least fortunate. In addition to paying taxes, they were obliged to perform two services for the state that were not only a nuisance but involved time, labor, and the consumption of their meager possessions. These were the military service and the transportation service. Not much can be said about the military service except that it was not much different from the universal military conscription practiced in other countries at the time. The transportation service was a particularly onerous burden for the poor *albatu.* The *albatus* were required to spend part of their time on duty at postal relay stations. Genghis Khan had introduced fast postal service in his empire, and his successors maintained relay stations at fixed points along the old mail routes. A certain number of *albatus,* together with their carts and animals (horses, camels, oxen), were on duty at all times at these stations. They picked up mail and official passengers as required and delivered mail and passengers to the next relay station, from which they were carried along another stretch of the road by still other *albatus* and their beasts of burden. Another form of transportation duty consisted of providing personnel and transport in nonrelay service—that is, *albatus* were obliged to pick up travelers and deliver them to any destination their masters demanded.

This system was a terrible strain on the limited resources of the *albatu,* who had to pay his taxes regularly—or irregularly, whenever special levies were introduced—and it put him in debt to such an extent that he was never able to extricate himself.

Justice in prerevolutionary Mongolia was administered by officials appointed by the government. There were two levels of justice: one for the nobility, another for the common people. Members of the nobility could be punished for various crimes, but they were tried without the use of persuasion. Confessions were usually obtained from commoners and peasants by the use of torture. If the sentenced criminals were members of the nobility, their sentences had first to be approved by the central authorities, but punishment was meted out to convicted commoners and peasants on the spot.

The legal system was based on custom and precedent. The state seldom initiated charges, either in civil or criminal cases. It was up to the victim to press charges, after which there was an investigation, in which a government official tried to bring both sides to a peaceful agreement. If that failed, the accused—if he was not a prince or a member of the nobility—was subjected to physical pressure. There were nine rungs to the torture ladder, each more formidable than the rung before it. The customary first step consisted of one hundred slaps with a wide leather strap across the face of the accused. If he stubbornly refused to confess, he was subjected to the second grade of torture, in which his buttocks were beaten with a stick about one and a half yards long. The maximum duration of this second form of torture was one hundred blows. If the accused still persisted in refusing to confess, he was forced to kneel on sharp stones for a prescribed period of time. Subsequent forms of torture were even more refined. The victim was suspended on ropes, or narrow bamboo splinters were inserted under his finger nails. The final steps up the torture ladder were the most heinous of all, and consisted of pouring molten lead into the palm of his hand and attaching red-hot coins to his back. The coins were Chinese ones with square openings through which special metal hooks could be inserted for the purpose of tearing out the flesh.

Only in exceptional cases were all nine forms of torture used. Usually, the accused broke down and confessed after the second or third step. Officials could easily be bribed by the accused or by his relatives, in which case the torture was a mere sham, and the accused, who suffered little or no pain, naturally refused to "confess." The bribed official then leveled charges against the plaintiff for making false accusations, and the plaintiff in turn was subjected to torture—real torture this time—in order to make him either withdraw the original accusations or confess that he had made false accusations.

Punishment varied with the crime. As a rule serious crimes were punished on the principle of a head for a head, an eye for an eye. For convicted murderers, this meant decapitation, although in later days, shooting was the means of execution. If the murderer was accused of killing his mother or father, he was executed only after undergoing a series of tortures.

Inflicting bodily harm was punishable by a prescribed number of lashes, by chaining by the neck, or by imprisonment, in addition to which the guilty party was required to pay damages and charges for medical attention required by the plaintiff. Robbery was also punished by lashes and imprisonment. In thievery cases, first offenders were given from twenty to thirty lashes and were made to repay the amount of the victim's loss. Most thefts were of animals. Cattle rustlers received double the initial punishment for the second offense and long-term prison sentences for repeated rustlings.

Mongols usually married at the age of 16 to 19. It did not matter which member of the union was the older, but it was vitally important that the union be concluded in accordance with provisions of the lunar calendar. According to this calendar, years were either weak or strong, and a man born during a weak (female) year was seldom permitted by the lamas to marry a girl born during a strong (male) year. In order to claim his bride, a prospective groom had first to "ransom" her from her family. The average ransom consisted of 30 to 40 ounces (*lan*) of silver and two horses. At the time the ransom was paid, meticulous arrangements were made for the prospective bride's dowry, which was to be paid in full one year after the wedding. The usual dowry consisted of two or three camels and from thirty to forty head of sheep. Another requirement was for the father of the groom to provide the skeleton structure and felt covering of the *yurt* of the newlyweds and for the bride's father to supply the ropes used to tie the felt strips to the tent's wooden skeleton, as well as the interior decorations.

The foundations of Mongolian society were firmly implanted in the family, consisting of a husband, one wife, and children. The husband was considered the head of the family. In case of the husband's death, the widow automatically became the head of the family until the eldest son came of age.

Monogamy was the custom, but there were exceptions, especially among the rich and privileged. Where polygamy was practiced, each wife would have a separate tent. There were no harems, or multiwife households as in Moslem society, and Mongolian women were not subservient to their husbands. A Mongolian wife's status was little different from that of her husband. A husband consulted his wife when an important decision was to be made. Either party was permitted to leave the other for any reasonable cause, and the marriage was perfunctorily dissolved after an amicable agreement had been reached on the division of communal property. In such a situation, the wife had equal rights with her husband, but a favorable outcome was largely dependent on the Mongolian lunar calendar.

The lunar calendar was introduced into Mongolia in 1027 and was based on cycles of sixty years each. The great sixty-year cycle consisted of five twelve-year cycles. There was a rather complicated system of designating each year in one of these twelve-year cycles. The first year was a mouse year; in addition it was called a strong, or male, year. The second year was named after a cow born with a tail as long as its horns; it was a female year. The third (male) year was the year of the tiger. The fourth (female) year was the year of the little lop-eared hare. Alternately male and female, the fifth year was the year of the mighty dragon; the sixth, the year of the snake; the seventh, the year of the swift-footed horse; the eighth, the year of the lamb. The last four years, were: the year of the monkey, the year of the hen, the year of the barking dog, and the year of the hog.

Each of the five minor twelve-year cycles of the sixty-year cycle was dedicated to one of the "elements" of nature—wood, fire, earth, iron, and water—and each of these natural elements was associated with a color. Fire was red, earth was yellow, iron was white, wood was blue, and water was black. This complicated system of designations makes it possible to pinpoint each year of a sixty-year cycle with precision. One could say that an event occurred in the year of the blue mouse (the first year of the first twelve-year cycle) or, that an event occurred in the year of the red cow (the second year of the second twelve year cycle—or the fourteenth year of the present sixty-year cycle).

Before the Communists came to power, the Mongolian lunar calendar exerted a tremendous influence on the lives of the people. The dates of births, marriages, deaths, and funerals were all interpreted according to their occurrence in the great or small cycles of the lunar calendar. Only one important holiday was celebrated in old Mongolia: the New Year's day of the lunar year, which might fall on any day in the months of February or March. This day, called *Tsagan Sar* (White Month), coincided with the advent of spring, according to the lunar calendar, the day when cattle started breeding. Old Mongols still remember

the great annual celebrations that marked the arrival of the
new lunar calendar year. The New Year's ritual was adhered
to by all the inhabitants of a settlement. The ceremony centered around the custom of tea drinking. When guests arrived, they were greeted by the lady of the *yurt,* who offered
them tea, after which the male head of the household offered
them the alcoholic *kumys.* Then both guests and hosts departed for a neighbor's *yurt,* where the same ceremony was
repeated, with perhaps a little vodka consumed in addition
to the tea and *kumys.* The process was repeated several times
with a steadily enlarging group. One can imagine the condition of the original guests after visiting every *yurt* in the
village!

Like so many ancient customs, this method of celebrating
the New Year is dying out in the cities and on the large collective farms of modern Mongolia, where the old lunar
calendar has been replaced by the Gregorian calendar.
Tsagan Sar no longer refers to the day on which the cattle
start breeding and giving milk. By government decree,
Tsagan Sar has been a holiday of labor and happiness since
1959.

The consumption of tea in Mongolia is not limited to the
New Year celebration. Tea drinking is important both in
the social life and in the domestic habits of the Mongols,
particularly in rural society.

Most travelers to Mongolia in prerevolutionary days agreed
that Mongols never drank cold, fresh water, preferring instead to drink their traditional tea. According to an age-old
custom, whenever a weary traveler comes to a nomad's *yurt,*
he is invited inside, made comfortable in a place of honor,
and immediately offered a cup of tea. It is considered as
much an insult not to be offered tea as it is for a guest to

refuse to drink the tea. In early times, when Mongols made pilgrimages to distant monasteries, they traveled light. There was always a *yurt* within riding distance where they could find shelter and quantities of tea, which not only quenched their thirst but satisfied their pangs of hunger. The reason for this is that the tea is like a tea soup.

Often tea was pressed into bricks about fourteen inches long, seven inches wide, and almost two inches thick. Centuries ago it was found that tea compressed into the shape of bricks was easier to transport, and there was less loss in transit. In preindependence days, Mongolia had no currency, and the hard, durable, uniformly shaped tea-bricks were used as a means of exchange and were often preferred in place of negotiable currency. It was quite common in those days to be paid ones' wages—or to pay one's debts—in brick tea.

The usual way Mongols prepare tea from bricks is to break off a piece and grind it in a wooden mortar with a pestle. The woman of the *yurt* places the ground tea in a pot of cold water, which is placed on the fire to boil. The tea is boiled for about ten minutes—no longer—and milk and sizable quantities of butter are added and salt to taste. It was formerly the custom for the hostess, after making a visitor comfortable and preparing the tea, to carry the first ladleful of tea outside the tent and sprinkle it on the ground to appease the spirits of the countryside. Only after the first ladle had been served to the spirits were the human occupants of the *yurt* served their tea. Kovalevsky, a nineteenth-century Russian traveler, was quite often a guest in Mongolian *yurts*. "After a cup or two of tea," he wrote, "your mind is refreshed and your body relaxed, and conversation flows freely."

The Mongolian custom of disposing of the dead often surprised outsiders. It was based on religious belief. A few departures from the customary "burial" have been noted, particularly when the bodies of important persons, such as princes, were to be disposed of. In such cases, the bodies were either cremated or placed on the ground and carefully covered with rocks to protect them from the attacks of animals and birds. But for most dead Mongols the procedure was different. The bodies of the dead were left on the plain to be consumed by wild beasts and birds. Like any Buddhist faith, the Lamaist religion taught that when a man died, his body should not be buried in the ground but should be given to the animals and birds and be consumed by them. An elaborate funeral ceremony preceded this act. The officiating lama would determine from his books the exact location of the spot on which the body should be placed and the direction the head should face. Since it was expected that the body would be torn to pieces by birds, wild dogs, and other animals, it was customary to dress the corpse in the oldest garments available. In rags hardly fit to wear, the body was carried to the prescribed spot and placed on the ground with a small cushion under its head and a Tibetan prayer book in its hands. The final act consisted in covering the body with a piece of cloth, kept in place by several rocks placed at each corner. The Mongolian funeral was then over, and the relatives departed. Wild dogs, waiting nearby, would quickly dispose of the body. The sooner the body was consumed by dogs and birds, the better, for this was taken as a sign that the spirit had departed without undue delay.

15 Foreign Relations

From the standpoint of foreign relations, the history of the Mongolian People's Republic can be divided into two, roughly equal periods. The first period lasted from the declaration of independence of the new republic in 1921 to the end of World War II. During this time, Mongolia's relations with the outside world were limited to contact with the Soviet Union. The period from the end of World War II to the present, however, has seen great changes in the structure of the countries of Europe and Asia, and Mongolia has at last taken her place among the nations of the postwar world.

For a quarter of a century after the new Mongolian state was formed, it lived in almost complete isolation. It was recognized diplomatically only by the Soviet Union. Not long after it came into being in 1921, the Mongolian People's Republic expressed a wish to have normal diplomatic relations with the other countries of the world. It did this formally in a declaration on September 14, 1921. The appeal was made to the United States as well as to other nonsocialist nations, but it fell on deaf ears. The other countries of the world did not consider Mongolia a truly independent state, capable of playing an international role. The response from Russia, however, was immediate, and, in October, 1921, the new Mongolian government sent a delegation to Moscow at the invitation of the Soviets to negotiate a treaty. The treaty of November 5, 1921, the first negotiated by the Mongolian People's Republic, formalized the friendly relations already existing between Mongolia and Russia. This agreement was based on principles of equality and mutual respect and acknowledged the recognition by the two countries of each other's independence. Mongolia's next major agreement with the Soviet Union was made in 1925. On the basis of the new agreement, the Soviet Union withdrew its troops from Mongolia. The Mongolian government had proved itself stable, and military assistance was no longer needed.

This situation did not last long. The political tensions and struggles that were to mark the 1930's and erupt into war before the decade was over began practically on Mongolia's doorstep with the occupation of Manchuria by Japanese troops in 1931. In the next few years, there were numerous border incidents between Japanese soldiers and Mongolian border guards. These threats forced Mongolia to seek the assurance of Soviet military aid in case of armed aggression by Japan. A so-called gentlemen's agreement was concluded between the Soviet Union and Mongolia on November 27, 1934, providing mutual assistance in the event of military aggression by a third party.

International tensions continued to increase. The pressure on the Manchurian border mounted. Eventually, Mongolia was forced to turn to Russia for additional assurances. These were forthcoming, and on March 12, 1936, a new ten-year agreement was signed. The new treaty was not a mere scrap of paper, as was proved when Japanese military forces invaded Mongolia in 1939 in the region of Khalkhin Gol. The foray turned into a major armed clash. The battle was joined by the Soviets, the Japanese were turned back. The situation along the Manchurian border was restored to normal by July, 1940.

The next important event concerned the recognition of Mongolia as an independent nation. On the basis of decisions arrived at during the Yalta Conference in 1945, the United States and Great Britain, under pressure from the Soviet Union, agreed to support the *status quo* in Mongolia. For all practical purposes, this was recognition of Mongolia's independence from China, which had been a sore point with the Chinese government from the beginning. Furthermore, it was agreed that a plebiscite would be conducted among the Mongolian people to learn whether they preferred independence to existence within the framework of Chiang Kai-shek's China. The plebiscite was conducted on October 20, 1945. There was no doubt about the outcome, and on January 5, 1946, China formally agreed to accept the fact of Mongolia's independence. Normal diplomatic relations were established between the two countries on February 14 of the same wear. A few days later, a Treaty of Friendship and Mutual Assistance was signed by Mongolia and the Soviet Union to replace the ten-year mutual assistance agreement, which had just expired. The new treaty pledged economic and cultural cooperation as well as military assistance, and with its signing Mongolia's foreign relations passed into their second, postwar, phase.

The days when the Soviet Union and Mongolia were the

world's only socialist states were over, and the newly spawned Communist countries of Europe and Asia began to beat a path to Mongolia's door. The first of these countries to establish diplomatic relations with Mongolia was the Korean People's Democratic Republic (North Korea). This took place on October 16, 1948. In the meantime, China had been undergoing a revolution of its own, and, a year later, on October 6, 1949, the new Chinese People's Republic followed Korea's lead in recognizing the Mongolian People's Republic. In 1950, diplomatic relations were established with six European countries: Poland (on April 16), Bulgaria (April 21), Czechoslovakia (April 25), Hungary (April 30), Rumania (May 5), and Albania (May 24). Further recognition had to wait until November 16, 1954, when the new Democratic Republic of Vietnam (North Vietnam) established relations with Mongolia. The next two years witnessed a series of agreements establishing relations with neutral countries—India (in 1955), and Burma, Yugoslavia, and Indonesia (in 1956). Another series of agreements was brought about by the establishment of several new independent states in Africa and Asia in the early 1960's. These included Guinea, Cambodia, Cuba, Nepal, Mali, Algeria, Afghanistan, and the United Arab Republic.

Mongolia had not won its fight for recognition until it had been admitted to the United Nations, and this was not possible without much pulling of strings and backstage maneuvering. In the end, the countries of the Western bloc agreed to accept Mongolia as a member of the family of nations only on condition that the Soviet Union and other members of the Soviet bloc admit the Islamic Republic of Mauritania, a newly independent state of West Africa. All parties agreed, and Mongolia became a full-fledged member of the United Nations in October, 1961. Today Mongolia maintains diplomatic relations with some forty countries.

A country's foreign trade is an index to its economic ties with the outside world. In recent years, the quantities of goods imported to and exported from Mongolia have increased by leaps and bounds. In the quarter-century between 1940 and 1964, for example, there was a sixfold increase in foreign trade.

During the early years of the young republic, foreign capital and foreign interests were still very much in evidence. In the middle 1920's, more than 80 per cent of Mongolia's export trade was in the hands of English, American, German, Russian, and Chinese firms. The Chinese controlled 60 per cent of this business, Anglo-American firms about 20 per cent. Russian enterprises accounted for only 3 per cent. Most of the remaining exports were controlled by Mongolian cooperatives and Soviet trading organizations. In 1927, foreign capital was responsible for about three-fourths of the export and half of the import business. This situation existed until 1930, when a state monopoly was introduced and strictly enforced. Foreign capital was completely eliminated from the economy, and from 1930 to the early 1950's Mongolia's foreign trade was conducted exclusively with the Soviets. This changed in 1953, when Mongolia signed a trade agreement with the Chinese People's Republic. Other agreements followed. In 1957, Mongolia maintained trade relations with eight Soviet-bloc countries. By 1962, the number had grown to seventeen, and in the next few years economic ties were made with several countries of the capitalist world. Today Mongolia has trade agreements with more than twenty countries.

Animal husbandry and its products are the backbone of Mongolia's economy. Almost 90 per cent of the country's exports are wool, cattle, meat, fat, grain, skins, hides, and furs. Imports are about two-thirds machinery and industrial equipment and one-third consumer goods. Sugar, tea, tobacco, and fruit are staple import items, but the trend is toward a decrease of imports of clothing, footwear, woolen materials, and other items that are being manufactured in increasing quantities in Mongolian factories by the Mongols themselves.

The Soviet Union is still Mongolia's largest source of imports and its most important customer, accounting for about three-fourths of the country's foreign trade. Machinery and heavy equipment account for about half of all imports from Russia; consumer goods account for a large part of the rest, but chemical products, paper, and textiles are being imported in sizable quantities.

Until recently, China was Mongolia's second largest trade partner. The exchange of goods was particularly lively in the years 1959 and 1960, the leading imports being food products (fruit and rice) and textiles (silk and cotton). In 1961–62, Sino-Soviet relations started to deteriorate, affecting relations of China and Mongolia to such an extent that trade with Mongolia fell off. The present rate of trade with China is only a trickle of what it was in the early 1960's.

Czechoslovakia has replaced China as Mongolia's second largest customer. It exports chiefly wool and supplies Mongolia with machinery and equipment, particularly for the leather and shoe industries, as well as with medicines and equipment for hospitals and medical institutions. The next most important East European participant in Mongolia's foreign trade is East Germany, which, in exchange for products of animal husbandry, supplies the country with textiles, cameras, sewing machines, radios, and equipment for diesel-operated power stations. Poland is not far behind East Germany. It supplies Mongolia with industrial products and textiles. Hungary, Bulgaria, and Rumania also participate in the exchange of goods. From Bulgaria come textiles, canned goods, and drugs. Hungary provides water-well–drilling equipment, machines, and medical equipment. Rumania supplies oil-well–drilling equipment and some chemical and textile products. All three countries receive in exchange Mongolian hides, skins, and furs. From North Korea, Mongolia imports silks, fruit, and the products of Korea's chemical industry. From North Vietnam come lumber, fruit, and rice.

Trade is not limited to the Soviet bloc. Quite lively trading relations are maintained with Switzerland, England, India, France, the United Arab Republic, and Japan. In 1967, this list was augmented by Austria, the Netherlands, Greece, and Yugoslavia. The new trade agreement with Japan states that Japan will receive, in exchange for auto tires, textiles, and consumer goods, Mongolian furs, tungsten, and other raw materials to the amount of $1 million annually for three years, at the end of which a new agreement is to be negotiated. The visit of President Tito of Yugoslavia to Mongolia in 1968 resulted in the signing of an agreement that provides for a 20 per cent increase in trade over 1967, an increase equivalent to $2 million. Yugoslavia is to supply Mongolia with textiles, paper products, synthetic fabrics, beverages, and items not otherwise available in Mongolia in exchange for wool, camel's hair, furs, hides, and animal husbandry products.

Mongolia, which for so long had been the most backward country in Asia, could hardly be expected to pull itself up to the economic levels of other nations without help. The only contributor to Mongolian economic development before World War II was the Soviet Union. After the war, recognition of Mongolia by other socialist and Communist nations led naturally to wider economic relations. Mongolia's membership in COMECON, the Council for Mutual Economic Assistance (which is composed of practically all member nations of the Soviet bloc), led not only to an increase in foreign trade but to an expanded program of economic aid. This help came as outright gifts and as goods and services on favorable long-term credit, meaning that either no interest was charged on loans or that the interest was a maximum of 2 per cent per annum.

The greatest contributor of aid for building up the postwar economy of Mongolia was the Soviet Union. Soviet assistance poured into Mongolia in an endless stream from 1947 to 1957. During this decade, long-term loans amounted to 900 million rubles. An additional 100 million rubles of industrial equipment brought the total of the ten-year aid program to more than 1 billion rubles, the equivalent of 1.1 billion U.S. dollars. Gifts to the Mongolian People's Republic consisted of the transfer of Soviet-constructed airports at Ulan Bator and Sayn Shanda in 1957, together with all airport equipment and several of the planes based at these airports. Construction and equipment provided on liberal long-term credit included a milk *kombinat* (dairy), flour mills, coal mines, electric power plants, expanded transportation and communication facilities, and modern heating and waterwork systems in the nation's capital.

The Soviet postwar program of economic assistance to Mongolia was regulated by several agreements, the first of which, having to do with economic and cultural cooperation, was signed in 1946. A 1959 agreement for the development of virgin lands provided for the sending to Mongolia of forty-seven Soviet engineers, sixty technicians, and two hundred tractor-drivers for a period of two years, not to mention assistance in the form of tractors and other agricultural machinery, all of which were supplied on very favorable terms.

On September 9, 1960, a new agreement was signed in Moscow providing economic and technical assistance for Mongolia's third five-year plan (1961–65). During these five years, the Soviet Union undertook construction of fifteen new industrial establishments, including a furniture factory and a "bread factory." Three grain elevators were built, oil fields were surveyed and developed, and power plants were constructed, as were power lines and pipelines. Facilities in industries that utilized the products of Mongolia's animal husbandry were enlarged. In 1966, when Mongolia was about to start on a fourth five-year-plan, another agreement on economic and technical cooperation between the countries was signed, covering the period 1966–70.

Needless to say, Russian aid has had an impact on Mongolian society, which has been permeated by Russian ideas and culture. The wife of Tsedenbal, the present Communist leader of Mongolia, is a Russian. The new alphabet adopted in 1945 is patterned on the Cyrillic alphabet used in Russia. Each year, thousands of Mongolian students attend classes in Russian universities. While altruism may be a motive in Soviet aid to Mongolia, sound political reasons are not lacking. During the years when China was governed by Chiang Kai-shek, Mongolia served as a buffer state between Russia and China, and there were unmistakable signs that the Soviets would look with favor on Mongolia's eventually joining the family of republics that makes up the Soviet Union. Paradoxically, any thought of Mongolia's becoming part of the Soviet Union was forgotten when Mao Tse-tung came to power in China. With the deterioration of relations between China and the Soviet Union, Soviet desire to preserve the integrity and independence of Mongolia has not diminished.

China until recently was the second largest contributor to the Mongolian aid program. The Chinese began by constructing a power plant, a wool-washing factory, and prefabricated houses. They helped to remodel and rebuild Ulan Bator and later built the Harhoron irrigation system, constructed highways and bridges, and contributed a paper factory and a lumber mill. Czechoslovakia did its share by setting up a footwear factory, building a plant for the processing of sheepskins and one for tanning hides and by undertaking to construct cement and leather factories that are expected to produce 200,000 tons of cement and to process 1.2 million pieces of goatskin per year. Equipment for a 200-bed hospital has also been provided by Czechoslovakia.

Other countries of Eastern Europe that have contributed significantly to Mongolia's over-all economic growth include Poland, which constructed a brick factory that manufactures 48 million fire-resistant bricks a year, a roofing plant, and a plant for the processing of cattle carcasses. East Germany reconstructed and enlarged the central printing shop in Ulan Bator, constructed a modern, fully mechanized meat-processing plant, and has recently signed an agreement calling for the construction of a new carpet factory in the Mongolian capital. Hungary and Bulgaria have provided economic aid but on a smaller scale. Hungary assisted in developing Mongolia's sewing machine and pharmaceutical industries and in developing water wells. Bulgaria's contribution has been to provide assistance in the development of Mongolia's agriculture.

16 Mongolia—Today and Tomorrow

Mongolia has made great strides in the last fifty years in industry and agriculture. The country's natural resources are just beginning to be energetically exploited. New cities and towns have been established. Mongols are growing grain and vegetables, but Mongolia is still dependent on the products of animal husbandry. The greatest proportion of the people are gainfully employed as herdsmen, the traditional occupation of the Mongols. They roam the steppes on horseback and migrate with their herds, and by and large, they still tend their horses, camels, cattle, sheep, and goats in the way of their ancestors. However, the Mongols can count on Soviet assistance.

During the winter of 1967–68, when severe cold gripped the country and temperatures of from 50 to 60 degrees below zero were not uncommon, there was a shortage of fodder. The Russians not only allocated tons of fodder but delivered it to the areas affected by the merciless weather, sometimes in motorized convoys, sometimes by making air drops from transport planes. According to a broadcast from Ulan Bator on April 1, 1968, 150 heavily loaded trucks left the capital for Bayan Hongor *aymag,* which has the country's highest concentration of livestock. It was the fifth convoy organized by the Soviets during that catastrophic winter. (Distance is an enemy to be overcome; one such convoy in 1964 had to cover 2,000 miles to deliver 1,000 tons of fodder to snowed-in grazing lands.) In addition to fodder, the Russians delivered hundreds of tons of dry milk and cod liver oil for the feeding of young animals. But even such massive attempts to relieve the starving herds are insufficient during such cold winters. Thousands of animals died from starvation and exposure during the winter of 1967–68, and it was necessary to slaughter 2.5 million more.

Lack of sufficient water for grazing animals and for agricultural purposes has stunted the country's economic growth for centuries. But this desolate picture is changing. The rivers and lakes of the north have begun to supply water for experimental irrigation projects, which will eventually allow for a wider distribution of cultivable land. Even more important are the numerous projects to provide the steppe lands with water from underground sources. If these sources can be tapped, there will probably be more than enough water for grazing cattle. Soviet hydrologists have been working on the problem for years, digging deeper wells and tapping artesian wells. In 1960, Hungary sent its first teams of water-research specialists into Mongolia to help locate underground water reservoirs and devise means for bringing these hidden supplies to the surface. The Hungarian effort has been concentrated in the southeastern part of the country, which has always been poorly supplied with natural wells. Many new underground reservoirs have been discovered, and new wells have been dug that now provide precious water to the grazing animals and to the farms in the area.

The fourth five-year plan (1966–70) includes ambitious plans for increasing the availability of water. By 1970, the Mongols plan to create about ten thousand watering stations in the dry lands, using state funds for the purpose. Ten thousand additional wells are to be built by the cooperatives, using their own funds and labor. Irrigation projects have been planned that will almost double the available grazing lands, and the 56 million acres now available for grazing are to be provided with improved and additional water supplies. This is indeed an ambitious plan for a country with such a small population, but, even if this goal is not attained, the country will have made an auspicious beginning in alleviating the water shortage.

The economic future of Mongolia, therefore, depends to a great extent on the elimination of the disastrous conditions brought on by severe winters and summer droughts. Sufficient fodder to feed the herds the year round must be stored, and efforts to locate and utilize all available water resources, both under and above ground, must be increased.

The increase in the number of Mongols who are attending elementary schools, vocational schools, *technicums,* and in stitutions of higher learning will have a beneficial effect on agriculture. Most of the educated Mongols become members of the skilled labor force, rather than herdsmen like their fathers. There is a gradual decrease in the number of nomadic horsemen, and perhaps the importance of animal husbandry in the Mongolian economy will diminish. The present system of animal husbandry will gradually change to a scientifically regulated type of husbandry, no longer dependent on grazing lands that are subject to disaster from blizzards or drought and needing fewer herdsmen attending the animals.

The industrial face of Mongolia is also changing, particularly in the field of light industry, such as the production of consumer goods, textiles, and foodstuffs. Heavy industry lags behind, but the trend to industrialization is evident in the new factories, the flour mills, the power plants, and other industrial enterprises. Several projects under way promise to make the country self-sufficient in petroleum and coal. Ulan Bator is rapidly becoming an industrialized city, and other industrial communities have sprung up—such as Nalaikha and Darkhan.

Politically, the future of Mongolia is inextricably intertwined with the outcome of the ideological struggle between its two mighty neighbors—the Soviet Union to the north and Red China to the south. The fact that Mongolia has sided with Russia in this struggle has subjected the country to verbal abuse from Mao's China. China has even hinted darkly that Mongolia, like Inner Mongolia, was an integral part of China before the Chinese revolution of 1911. It seems that only the determination of the Soviet Union to defend Mongolian independence has prevented China from swallowing up Mongolia. China's efforts to build Mongolian industry have mostly been suspended. Chinese workers and technicians have been called home. Trade with China, which was at one time second only to Mongolia's trade with the Soviet Union, has been reduced, and the 1968 agreement regarding the exchange of goods between the two countries is a pale reflection of normal trade relations.

However, Russia has often taken more than a friendly

interest in Mongolia. Had the Chiang Kai-shek government remained in power in China, the Soviet Union probably would have added the Mongolian People's Republic to its collection of autonomous republics, a plan the rise to power of Mao Tse-tung rendered no longer feasible.

One million Mongols surrounded by a billion Russians and Chinese makes for a precarious present, but there is no reason why Mongolia cannot retain her independence under these conditions, even if it must resort to playing one neighbor against the other. For obvious reasons, Mongolia will always be culturally and economically oriented toward Russia, so the Mongols may never be completely free to determine their own foreign policy. However, now that diplomatic recognition by both Communist and non-Communist countries has ended the country's former isolation and a general thaw in the climate of all Communist nations seems to have set in, there is little doubt that, by and large, Mongolia will be able to shape its own destiny without assistance or tutelage from either of its Communist neighbors. Mongols are Mongols first and Communists and Soviet sympathizers second. By virtue of their isolation and their traditions, they are sturdily nationalistic. In 1958, an Englishman, Charles Bawden, wrote in *The Manchester Guardian:*

These forty years have cost the Mongols a heavy price for their progress. . . . Unimaginative obedience to Communist theory under Stalinist guidance brought the country near disaster. . . . The Russians have nearly all gone since the completion of the Moscow-Peking railway, though a few technicians and a very few soldiers remain. . . .

It is not enough appreciated in the West that Mongolia is an independent country. What is being done there is being done by the Mongols for themselves, not as agents of any other power, though of course it is true that they are a million people between the huge might of Russia on one side and China on the other, and as long as these two powers agree Mongol independence is to them innocuous. The Mongols form a vigorous ethnic group, vividly conscious of their historical identity. . . .

Outwardly public life is patterned on the Soviet model, but one very soon realizes that the Mongols are first and always Mongols, independently thinking as far as their incredible physical isolation permits them, conscious of their national identity and doing their utmost to preserve it in language, art, and historical studies.

The independence of Mongolia, backed by the might of the Soviet Union, seems more or less assured for the immediate future. The country has one very important prerequisite for growth and progress—a small but growing and developing population in an enormous area with abundant, if rather unevenly distributed, natural resources. Barring social or economic upheavals, the Mongols will continue to exploit these resources, to create new industries, to improve their living standards, to expand their agriculture, and eventually to overcome the climatic and seasonal hazards that have threatened their migrating herds since the days of Genghis Khan.

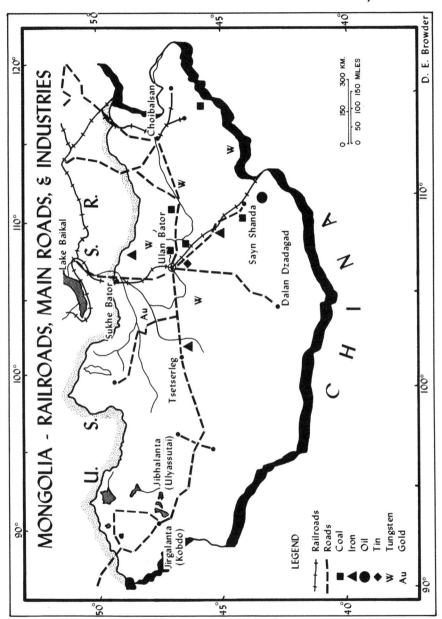

MONGOLIA - RAILROADS, MAIN ROADS, & INDUSTRIES

LEGEND

Railroads
Roads
Coal
Iron
Oil
Tin
Tungsten
Gold

D. E. Browder

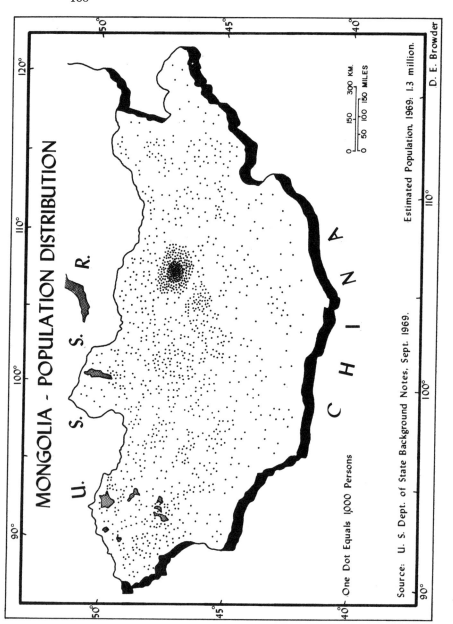

MONGOLIA - POPULATION DISTRIBUTION

U. S. S. R.

C H I N A

One Dot Equals 1,000 Persons

Source: U. S. Dept. of State Background Notes, Sept. 1969.

Estimated Population, 1969: 1.3 million.

D. E. Browder

300 KM.
150
0

150 MILES
100
50
0

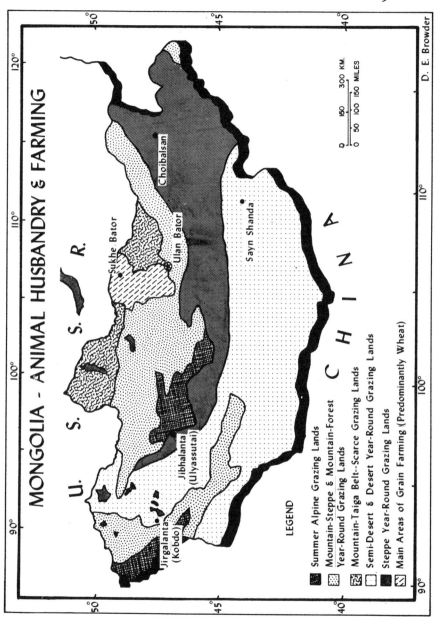

MONGOLIA - ANIMAL HUSBANDRY & FARMING

U. S. S. R.

C H I N A

Choibalsan

Sukhe Bator

Ulan Bator

Sayn Shanda

Jibhalanta
(Ulyassutai)

Jirgalanta
(Kobdo)

D. E. Browder

0   150   300 KM.
0 50 100 150 MILES

LEGEND

Summer Alpine Grazing Lands

Mountain-Steppe & Mountain-Forest
Year-Round Grazing Lands

Mountain-Taiga Belt--Scarce Grazing Lands

Semi-Desert & Desert Year-Round Grazing Lands

Steppe Year-Round Grazing Lands

Main Areas of Grain Farming (Predominantly Wheat)

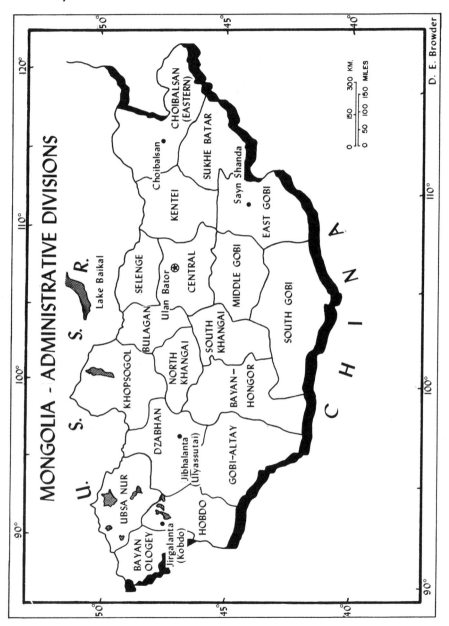

MONGOLIA - ADMINISTRATIVE DIVISIONS

U. S. S. R.

Lake Baikal

CHOIBALSAN (EASTERN)

Choibalsan

SUKHE BATAR

KENTEI

Sayn Shanda

EAST GOBI

SELENGE

Ulan Bator

CENTRAL

MIDDLE GOBI

SOUTH GOBI

BULAGAN

KHOPSOGOL

NORTH KHANGAI

SOUTH KHANGAI

BAYAN– HONGOR

DZABHAN

Jibhalanta (Ulyassutai)

GOBI–ALTAY

UBSA NUR

HOBDO

BAYAN OLOGEY

Jirgalanta (Kobdo)

C H I N A

D. E. Browder

300 KM.

150

150 MILES

100

50

0

Suggested Reading

Andrews, Roy Chapman. *The New Conquest of Central Asia.* New York: The American Museum of Natural History, 1932. An authoritative report of scientific expeditions to Mongolia in the 1920's. Numerous photographs and good maps showing routes of the Central Asian Expedition, which culminated in discovery of dinosaur eggs.

Bisch, Jorgen. *Mongolia: Unknown Land.* New York: Dutton, 1963. A popular description of the results of two recent trips across Mongolia. Many color photographs.

Charol (Prawdin), Michael. *The Mongol Empire: Its Rise and Legacy.* London: Allen & Unwin, 1952. A thorough treatment of the subject.

Hedin, Sven. *Riddles of the Gobi Desert.* New York: Dutton, 1933. A very interesting report of the experiences of this famous Swedish explorer and scholar. A scholarly but popularly written book.

Heissig, Walther. *A Lost Civilization: The Mongols Rediscovered.* New York: Basic Books, 1966. A rather haphazard description of Mongolia and its people. Nevertheless, it gives much information and a good picture of the present day Mongolia.

Jackson, W. A. Douglas. *Russo-Chinese Borderlands*. Princeton: Van Nostrand, 1962. Although the book is concerned with the entire Russo-Chinese border, it also touches extensively on the status of Mongolia. An expertly written treatise on the subject by a well-known American geographer.

Jisl, Lumir. *Mongolian Journey*. London: Batchworth Press, 1960. This popular description of Mongolia has only 16 pages of text, but it contains 127 pages of excellent black-and-white photographs.

Lattimore, Owen. *Mongol Journeys*. London: Jonathan Cape, 1941. A good book by a recognized authority of Mongolia, describing the country in the late 1930's.

————. *Nationalism and Revolution in Mongolia*. New York: Oxford University Press, 1955. This book consists of two parts: Lattimore's description of events that led to the growth of nationalism and to the revolution in Mongolia, and a description of the *Life of Sukhe Bator* by Sh. Nachukdorji, a Mongolian writer.

————. *Nomads and Commissars*. New York: Oxford University Press, 1962. An up-to-date description of present-day Mongolia and its people.

Micheli, Silvio. *Mongolia: In Search of Marco Polo and Other Adventures*. New York: Harcourt, Brace & World, 1967. Description of the travels of the Italian explorer, who came to Mongolia to follow the old route of Marco Polo.

Ossendowski, Ferdinand. *Beasts, Men, and Gods*. New York: Dutton, 1931. An exciting story of adventures of the author, who in his Mongolian travels came face to face with the Baron Ungern von Sternberg.

Ovdienko, Ivan Kh. *Economic-Geographical Sketch of the Mongolian People's Republic*. Bloomington, Ind.: The Mongolia Society,

1965. A good description of physical and economic geography of the country, its population, agriculture and animal husbandry, as well as of various branches of industry.

Polo, Marco. *The Travels of Marco Polo.* London: The Folio Society, 1958. Personal experiences of the thirteenth-century traveler in Mongolia, who spent more than twenty years in the Orient.

Poppe, Nicholas. *Introduction to Mongolian Comparative Studies.* Helsinki: Suomalais-Ugrilainen Seura, 1955. An excellent book for those who are interested in the study of comparative Mongolian linguistics.

Rupen, Robert A. *Mongols of the Twentieth Century.* Bloomington, Ind.: Indiana University Publications, 1964. A general description of the land and its people during three periods: before 1917, 1917–21, and the Soviet period.

Sandag, Sh. *The Mongolian Struggle for National Independence and the Building of a New Life.* Ulan Bator: State Publishing House, 1966. A glance at Mongolia from the point of view of a native of present-day Mongolia. This description covers prerevolutionary Mongolia, the birth of the people's Mongolia, consolidation of power, and finally, a description of the Mongolian People's Republic.

Tang, Peter S. H. *Russian and Soviet Policy in Manchuria and Outer Mongolia, 1911–1931.* Durham, N.C.: Duke University Press, 1959. A scholarly review of the play of power politics between China and Russia with regard to Mongolia and Manchuria.

Index

Adriatic Sea, 22
Agriculture: 88–97; animal husbandry, 93–96; collectivization, 89–93
Agrimba, 140
Albania, 62, 153
Albatu, 141–42
Alexander the Great, 22
Altaic linguistic group, 106–7
Amor, 59
Andrews, R. C., 167
Angara River (Siberia), 16
Arats, 107, 108
Arctic Ocean, 15–16
Arts and recreation, 123–37; ballet, 130; folk dancing, 128–30; folk singing, 128–30; literature, 126–28; movies, 130–31; *Nadom,* 132–35; Olympic Games of *1964,* 132; opera, 131; painting and sculpture, 131–32; Soviet-style national theater, 128; traditional and new sports, 132–35; wild-animal hunting, 135–37
Aymags, 64–65

Baikal, Lake (Siberia), 7–8, 22; Buryat inhabitants of, 7–8

Bator, Sukhe, 47–49, 52–57; industrial city named after, 81, 83, 87, 101, 109
Batu Khan, 29–34
Bavasan, 57–58
Bawden, Charles, 165–66
Bielgee, 129–30
Bisch, Jorgen, 167
Black Sea, 26
Bodo, 56, 67
Bogi Altai, 12
Brick tea, 4–5, 147–49
Buir Nur, 17, 85
Bukhara (Soviet Union), 26
Bulgaria, 153, 156, 160
Bulgun River region, 20
Burma, 37, 153

Caesar, Julius, 22
Caspian Sea, 25, 26
Chahar Province (China), 35
Charol, Michael, 167
Chiang Kai-shek, 152, 159, 165
Chin Empire (northern China), 24–25, 30
China, Communist, 19, 101–2, 153–55, 159
China, Imperial, 6, 45
China, Nationalist, 51

Chinese Eastern Railway, 98
Chinese Revolution of *1911,* 6,
  53, 54, 164
Choibalsan, 48, 49, 67–68; as dedicated Marxist revolutionary,
  52–54; his emulation of Stalin,
  58–60; industrial city named
  after, 81, 99, 101, 109; "personality cult" of, 60, 68; suc-
  ceeds Sukhe Bator, 57
Climate, 13–15
Collectives, 89–93; agricultural cooperatives, 91–92; and increased
  mechanization of agriculture,
  92–93; and state farms, 90–91
COMECON (Council for Mutual
  Economic Assistance), 80, 157
Communications and transportation, 98–105
Communist ideological struggle,
  164
Constitution of *1960,* 65
Council for Mutual Economic Assistance (COMECON), 80, 157
Cyrillic alphabet, 115, 125, 158
Czechoslovakia, 78, 82, 87, 153,
  155, 159

Dalan Dzadagad, 14, 79, 101
Damdinsuren, Ts., 126, 128
Danzan, 57–58
Dargomizhsky, A., 131
Darkhan, industrial complex at,
  76, 80–81, 109, 164
Deli, 112
Demid, Marshal, 59
Dorji, Damba, 58
Drofa, 20
Dzabkan River, 17
Dzunbayn, oil extraction at, 79–
  80, 83

East Germany, 87, 155–56, 159–
  60

Eastern Sayan Mountains (Siberia), 12, 18
Economy of Mongolia, 70–76,
  155. *See also* Five-year plans
Education: elementary, 115;
  higher, 116
Erdeni-Tsu monastery, 119–20

Farming, 96–97
Five–year plans, 71–73, 158, 163

Gabji, 140
Gegen, Bogdo, 47, 49
Gendun, Prime Minister, 59
Genghis Khan, 21–28. *See also*
  Temuchin
Georgia, Knights of, 26
Gobi Desert, 12, 13
Gobi region, 13, 18
Gobi rhubarb, 19
Golden Horde, 29–34, 41
Great Khingan Range, 16

Hara Nur, 17
Hara River, 16
Hara Usa, 17
Harbin (China), 15
Harhoron irrigation system, 159.
  See also Communist China
Hedin, Sven, 167
Heissig, Walther, 167
Hindu Kush, 40
Hirgis Nur, 17
Hsu Shu-cheng, General, 46
Hulagu, 35, 36, 38
Hungary, 83, 153, 156, 160, 162

India, 42, 153
Indochina, 37
Industries, 77–87; building materials, 81–82; chemicals, 83;
  coal, 77–79; commercial hunting, 84; cooperative, 85; electric power, 80–81; fishing, 85;

food, 85–86; light, 87; lumber, 82–83; mining other than coal, 83–84; oil, 79–80
Inner Mongolian Autonomous Region of China, 7, 45, 125
Irkutsk (Soviet Union), 103
Islam, 118
Izheslavets, 31

Jackson, W. A. Douglas, 168
Japan, 36
Japanese Kwantung Army, 50, 99, 152
Java, 37
Jisl, Lumir, 168
Juji, 29, 30

Kaganovich, Lazar, 63
Kalgan-Urga-Kyakhta route, 98
Kang-Teh, Emperor, 50–51
Karakorum, 27, 28, 109
Kazakhs (Bayan Ulegey Kazakh national *aymag*), 107
Kentei Range, 12, 16
Kerulen River, 16, 82, 89
Khalkha Mongols of Eastern Mongolia, 43–44. *See also* Mongolian People's Republic
Khalkha River, 16
Khalkin Gol River, Battle of, 50, 99, 152
Khamjilga, 141
Khangai, 12
Khangai Range, 12, 16, 18
Khitans, 22
Khorezm, 25–26, 40
Khorons, 64–65
Khoshuns, 138–140
Khrushchev, Nikita, 63, 65
Khubsugul Lake region, 17, 18, 20, 82, 84, 85. *See also* Soils and vegetation
Khural, 49, 65–66, 133

Kiev (Russia), 31–33
Kirghiz tribes, 22
Knock Noor Depression, 11
Kobdo River, 17, 20
Kozelsk (Russia), 33
Kublai Khan and Yuan Dynasty in China, 5–6, 35–37, 39
Kumys, 95, 112, 133, 135
Kurultai, 29–30, 32
Kyakhta congress of *1921,* 55–57, 60

Labor force, changes in composition of, 74
Lama Rebellion of *1932,* 50, 90
Lamaism, Mongolian, 36, 118–120, 139–40; celibacy of lama class in, 119; its influence undermined, 119–20; its monasteries formerly carriers of culture, 119; as outgrowth of Tibetan Buddhism, 118
Lattimore, Owen, 168
Lenin, Vladimir, 66, 126
Liegnitz, Battle of, 33
Lodoidamba, Ch., 128

Maksarjab, 54–55
Malacca, 37
Mamelukes of Egypt, 39–40
Manchus, 44–45
Mao Tse-tung, 159, 165
Mauritania, 51, 153
Mayagmar, O., 132
Micheli, Silvio, 168
Middle East, 41–42
Ming Dynasty in China, 37
Minjur, 132
Molotov, V., 63
Monastery of Choydzhin-Lama, 119
Mongolian Academy of Sciences, 89, 117–118
Mongolian Altai Range, 12, 18

Mongolian Art Exhibition of 1967, 131–32
Mongolian People's Republic, 43–45, 57; and Communist satellites, 153; friendly relations with Soviet Russia, 150–52; recognition of independence from China, 152; and Third World, 153
Mongolian People's Revolutionary party, 55, 68–69; internal struggles and purges, 59, 68; membership in, 68–69
Mongolneft Oil Company, 79
Monogamy, 145
Morin-khuur, 129
Moscow, 103, 104
Mothers' Glory medals, 120–121

Nachukdorji, Sh., 168
Nalaikha coal field, 73–74, 77, 78; growth of industrial center at, 109, 164
Namdag, D., 128
Napoleon, 22
Nationalism, 165–66
Natsagdorj, D., 126, 128
Nerguy, 129–30
North Korea, 19, 153, 156
North Vietnam, 19, 103, 153, 156
Novgorod (Russia), 32

Ochir, D. Tomor, 127–28
Ogadai, 29, 30, 33–34
Oirats of Western Mongolia, 43–44, 64. See also Sinkiang-Uighur Autonomous Region of China
Ongin Gol, 17
Onon River, 16, 23, 89
Orkhon River, 16, 82, 89
Ossendowski, Ferdinand, 168
Ovdienko, Ivan Kh., 168–69

Pacific Ocean, 15–16

Peking, 15, 24, 39, 45, 103, 104
Permafrost, 15
Poland, 78, 82, 153, 156, 159
Polo, Marco, 6
Poppe, Nicholas, 169
Prague, 104
Prerevolutionary living standards, 112–14; disease and high death rate, 112; lack of hygiene, 112–13; modern health services, 114; training of doctors and nurses, 114
Professional training, 117
Przhevalsky horses, 20, 135
Pskov (Russia), 32

Revsomol, 59
Rinchino, 57–58
Role of women, 121–22
Rumania, 153, 156
Rupen, Robert A., 169
Russian Revolution, 6
Ryazan (Russia), 31, 32

St. John, Knights of, 42
Samarkand, 26, 43
Sandag, Sh., 169
Sayn Shanda, 78–80, 101, 109, 157
Selenga River, 16, 82, 89
Shabinar, 141
Sharyn Gol, Adunchulum open-pit coal mine at, 76
Sinkiang-Uighur Autonomous Region of China, 45
Soils and vegetation, 18-19
Somons, 64–65
Soviet Union: cultural impact of, 128, 130–31, 158; massive economic and technical assistance from, 80, 92–93, 97, 158; its role in wiping out illiteracy, 115–116
Stalin, Joseph, 59, 60, 126–27

State farms, 91
Subutai, 26, 29–31
Sung Empire (south China), 6, 25, 30, 37

Tabun Bogdo Uula, Mount, 11–12
Taijai, 138–39
Tamerlane, 39–43
Tang, Peter S. H., 169
Tanguts, 24, 27, 28
Tarbagan, 20, 84, 137
Tchaikovsky, Peter I., 131
Temuchin, 23–24
Tien Shan Range, 40
Tientsin (China), 15
Tito visit of *1968*, 156
Toghon-Timur, 37–38
Tokhtamysh, 41
Tovshur, 129
Traditional society, 138–49; burials in, 149; marriage in, 144–45; predominance of lama theocracy in, 139; social classes in, 138; three classes of serfs in, 141–42; and use of lunar calendar, 145–47; and use of torture ladder, 142–44
Trans-Mongolian Railroad, 7, 78, 80, 83, 100, 101
Trans-Siberian Railway, 98, 99
Transcaucasia, 26, 41
Transportation and communications, 98–105
Tripartite Agreement of *1915*, 45–46
Troitskosavsk (Soviet Union), 47, 48. *See also* Kyakhta congress of 1921
Tsagan Sar, 146–47
Tsedenbal, 52, 60-63, 69
Tsende, L., 62

Tsevelsuren, 131
Tukhachevsky, Marshal, 59
Tuyin and Baydarag rivers, 17

Uigurs, 21–22, 24
Ulambayar, U., 128
Ulan Bator, 81, 83, 86, 87, 109, 115–17, 120, 126, 157; concentration of urban population in, 109; Gandan Tekchinling monastery in, 120; Mongolian State Publishing House in, 126; State University at, 117
Ulus, 30
Unen (Mongolian *Pravda*), 125–26
United Nations, Mongolia's entry into, in *1961*, 51, 154
Upsa Nur, 17
Urga, 46–49, 53, 55, 73
Uspensky Cathedral (Russia), 32

Valley of Great Lakes, 12–13, 17
Vladimir (Russia), 31–33
Von Sternberg, Baron Ungern, 6, 46–48

Water, shortage of, 17, 88–89, 162-63
Winter of *1967–68*, 161–62

Yablonovoy Range (Siberia), 12
Yadamsuren, U., 132
Yalta Conference, 51, 152
Yenisei River (Siberia), 16, 22
Yesukai, 23
Yoroo River, 16
Yurts, 82; as dominant form of rural housing, 109–11

Zhamtsarano, 57–58
Zorgal Khairkhan Mountains, new tungsten mine opened in, 84